Becoming a Firefighter

Additional books by author:

Firehouse Fraternity Oral History Series:
Volume II: Life Between Alarms
Volume III: Equipment
Volume IV: Responding
Volume V: Riots to Renaissance
Volume VI: Changing the NFD

The Newark Riots: A View from the Firehouse

An Eerie Silence: An Oral History of Newark
Firefighters at the WTC

Hervey's Boys: New Jersey's First Chinese Community
1870-1886 (And What Happened After That)

Fiction:
The Firebox Stalker
The Hand Life Dealt you
A-zou: A Woman Living in Interesting Times

Children's Fiction:
A Hundred Battles (YA)
A Broken Glass (YA)
Balancing Act (Middle Grade)

The Firehouse Fraternity

An Oral History of the
Newark Fire Department

Volume I

Becoming a Firefighter

Neal Stoffers

Springfield and Hunterdon Publishing
Copyright 2007
www.newarkfireoralhistory.com

First Printing: 2007

ISBN: 978-1-970034-06-6

Springfield and Hunterdon Publishing
East Brunswick, NJ 08816-5852

Dedicated to past, present, and future generations of Newark firefighters, and especially to the 67 firefighters who made the ultimate sacrifice upholding their oath to protect the lives and property of Newark's citizens.

Contents

Acknowledgements

The credit for much of this book goes to the members of the Newark Fire Department who gave so generously of their time to take part in my oral history project. The hours of recorded conversations they contributed will help preserve the history of Newark's fire department and of Newark itself. A list of those interviewed appears at the end of the book. This is their story. I am honored to tell it.

Foreword

This book is one of six which recount the experiences of Newark firefighters. Beginning with the memories of a firefighter appointed in 1942, they tell the story of New Jersey's largest city and her fire department as seen through the eyes of the men manning her firehouses. I have attempted to group related subjects together to give the reader a true feel for various aspects of the fire service. The comments of the men I interviewed are presented in order of appointment date. This method is an attempt to give a better picture of the chronology of the dramatic changes which occurred in the city of Newark and the fire service in general.

The seeds of these books were unknowingly planted in a small firehouse on Springfield Avenue and Hunterdon Street. It was here as a young firefighter that I sat in the kitchen of Six Engine and listened to conversations between veteran firefighters, captains, and Deputy Chiefs about a city and fire department that existed in another time.

In June of 1991, I began an oral history project to preserve the memories of these men and the generations of firefighters who followed. The purpose of this project was to capture not only the words, but the texture of their experiences. What was a firefighting career like during this period in Newark and by extrapolation in America? Fire departments across the country have shared the experiences of the NFD in one way or another. Whether read by a professional firefighter from New York City or by a volunteer firefighter from a small rural community, the stories will be familiar. The fire service is a small world with a common purpose.

It is hoped what is recorded here will show both a bygone era and the evolution of the Newark Fire Department into its present form. If others outside the fire service walk away with a better understanding of the firefighters and the fire departments that protect them, my time over the past years will have been well spent.

Chapter One: The City

Fredette: (appointed 1942) The city wasn't bad. The people weren't bad. When we would shovel hydrants, they would come out and bring us coffee at three o'clock in the morning. In those days they had to go out and shovel hydrants to make passes for the Ahrens Foxes to get in. We'd make a big V in the street. They would come out with coffee and things like that.

Then the people in the neighborhood, they use to close our doors. We were the last ones in the city to get overhead doors. We had the ones that closed by hand, the collapsible doors. They would come over and close our doors in the wintertime. We were the busiest company in the city and we were the last ones to get an oil burner. We still had the old fashion furnace and we had a little pot stove. We had a job trying to keep that stove hot.

They called the area around Six Engine *Shmierkase* County. That was all solid Germans. Then way around the Polish came up. They were down below Belmont Avenue. The Polish people came up from down neck, around Pulaski Street, St. Casimir's Church. Then the Irish and the Italians came in pretty heavy. The Italians went up to Vailsburg. From Vailsburg they went to up Livingston. They're still up in Livingston yet. But a lot of them came from Fairmont Avenue, Camden Street, down in that section.

The people and the forms of entertainment that we had in those days were great. We had all the parks. You could go down to the park and play football or play baseball. You didn't have to worry about being knocked off. We had Olympic Park where you could go swimming. We had Dreamland Park. You had a lot of recreation. Then you had Newark Bears stadium. We had a lot of YMCAs, the Hebrew Club on High Street, night professional basketball games. Then we had fights at the Laurel Garden.

We had the Velodrome. We had fights on Thursday nights. We had the Roller Dome. Years ago there was a lot of entertainment in Newark.

Vetrini: (appointed 1946) Newark was beautiful, beautiful. It had everything there. We had the show houses, the nightclubs, and the restaurants. It was very homey. Your neighborhood, people were out in the street in the evenings. Kids out playing stickball like we used to play, but you can't do that with cars today. It was beautiful. But gradually we had no choice. You couldn't find places in the city. And then with the G.I. loan, for two hundred and fifty dollars you buy a house. And for the two hundred and fifty dollars we went to the credit union, because we didn't have two hundred and fifty dollars. So, I moved out of the city, which was against the rules. We had no other choice.

You even had trouble getting a mortgage when you went to buy a house in the city. They wanted a large down payment. The banks were not giving the mortgages out. You could get a G.I. loan. You could get that. But then you had to get that down payment. Where are you going to get the down payment? We went out of the city. I went out of the city in 1951. For a ten thousand five hundred dollar house, I put down two hundred and fifty dollars. I paid forty two dollars a month mortgage, ninety dollars a year for heating, and the taxes were a hundred and forty dollars a year.

Redden: (appointed 1947) I was born in Newark and lived in Newark until I retired. I lived in the Clinton Hill section, Seymour Avenue, Chadwick Avenue. Went to Blessed Sacrament Grammar School, South Side High School, I guess now known as Shabazz. They were good schools at that time. Newark was a great town, four hundred and ten thousand population, theaters downtown. I used to spend my weekends down in

Weequahic Park. They had boat races on the lake, trotting races. They had a regular stadium there with the trotters. I used to like to go through the barns and visit with the horses. They had semi-pro baseball and they would attract three to four thousand people on weekends. So, there was so much to do. The theaters downtown, there were good restaurants in town, transportation was great, the bus system by Public Service. So, it was fine. I enjoyed myself thoroughly in Newark.

Clinton Hill was predominantly Irish and German. It was a great neighborhood. Clean, I lived in a three-story frame. I remember Saturday morning the women washing the front porches off, the front stoop. And of course at that time hardly anybody had an automobile. There was lots of room at the curb, if you did have an automobile, to park it. But the neighborhoods were great. I went to Bergen Street playground, spent most of my time there playing softball, paddle tennis. In fact, I played with some of the guys who were on the job with me. We all went on at the same time.

You could go anyplace in the city from Clinton Hill. You had theaters downtown where you had first run motion pictures and you also had the big bands coming in to the Adams. Good restaurants. You could walk anyplace in the City when I was growing up. You had no problem what so ever. Weequahic Park was a gathering place on the weekends. Thousands of people would go down there to see boat races on Saturday, trotting races. They had a nice stadium. I'm sure there was betting going on. And the baseball games, again they would have three thousand people, pass the hat around. Westside Park had a big pond with gold fish in it.

Kinnear: (appointed 1947) I don't think I had any impression then because I was living there, it was everything. But thinking back it was a great city. It had everything. I lived on Dewey Street. From Dewy Street I could walk half a block for church or for where I went to school. I could walk there and get a bus for downtown Newark or New York. There were neighborhood movies. There was the Hawthorne Theater, the Roosevelt Theater. The Roosevelt was on Clinton Avenue. The Hawthorne was on Hawthorne Avenue. The Park Theater was on Bergen Street. There was a couple up in Irvington I could even walk to without any problems. They built a Shop-rite store on Lyons Avenue and that was in my backyard. So, for shopping you could just walk around the corner and go shopping in a big supermarket. The city was great at that time. Of course, I didn't realize it or even think about it. But looking at the changes that have occurred, it was a great city, really. Downtown they had the Paramount, Proctors, and Bradford Theater, where they had top run films and stage shows. They had Lewy Prima. I don't think Sinatra ever came to Newark. Big bands, Tommy Dorsey, Jimmy Dorsey they played down there. So everything was there and within walking distance or bus ride. I think it was a nickel bus ride.

I would say it was at least eighty, eighty-five percent white at that time. There was a black neighborhood, which consisted of around Belmont Avenue, Prince Street, and maybe ran down to High Street, maybe from Springfield Avenue or Court Street over to Avon. But it was the black area. Basically the rest city, as far as I know, was white. I'd say eighty-five percent white, maybe even ninety percent white. North Newark was the Italian section. Vailsburg was where most of the Police and Firemen seemed to live. The section I lived in, the Weequahic section or Clinton Hill section, was mostly Jewish, a lot of rich Jewish. You know, doctors and lawyers. I don't know how we got in there. We were on the fringe though. Weequahic was really south of Lyons Avenue. We lived just a little bit north of Lyons Avenue. We were on the fringe, but that was mostly a

Jewish section. I guess down neck was a mixture. I didn't go down there too much, so I don't really know.

Masters: (appointed 1947) I was born and raised in Newark on four twenty-seven South Tenth Street, the house is gone now. I went to public schools, graduated West Side during the Depression. My dad and all these foreign born, they believed in education. There were no jobs. He said, "You go to vocational school." So, I went to Irvington vocational school. From Tenth Street, we walked every morning. It was a group of fellows. We would start from Bruce Street, as they came up the group got larger and larger. It was about forty, fifty fellows going there, Irvington vocational and we walked every day. At that time the bus fare was a nickel. Who had the nickel?

I took a general course, machine shop, carpentry, electric, everything. That came in handy later on. I graduated there. When I went looking for a job it was, "Oh, you need experience." How can I get experience if you won't hire me? So, at the time, President Roosevelt signed a bill creating the CC camps. You may have read about it, all over the country. I went down to the Sussex Avenue armory on Sussex Avenue. It's gone now and I signed up. The guy said, "Where do you want to go?" I said, "I want to go out west." Utah. I spent two years in Utah. You know where Bowab, Utah is? You know where the four states come together? Southeast corner of Utah, I stayed there two years. We were paid well. We were paid thirty dollars a month, but twenty-five dollars went home to your family, your mother and dad and you kept five dollars. Actually, you could use that money, but you're out in the desert. How can you use those five dollars?

It was all good training. When you were in camp, you were under the jurisdiction of the Army. But when you were out in the field working, making roads, or bridges over streams, planting trees, cutting trees down, you were under the jurisdiction of the Department of Agriculture. When you came back into camp, you had to change into Army uniform. Stood at attention while the flag was lowered and they played retreat and all that stuff. There were a lot of fellows in the Depression, especially from the south, they didn't know how to read or write. In fact, some of those southern boys never wore shoes. It was compulsory for them to go to class at night, three times a week. Learn how to write, read, what ever they lacked in. But I took up photography and typing. That was it.

The city of Newark was beautiful when I was a kid. Downtown Newark, they were all beautiful stores, high class stores too. You had Bamberger's. You had Macy's. You had Orhbach's. You had all these good men's clothing stores. It was a beautiful city. My father worked downtown. He was with the Street Department.

When I came on the job in '47, the city was still good. It was still beautiful. The makeup in my day was white, Italians in the North Ward. Every section had its own ethnic group. You go to the South Ward, it was Jewish. East Ward was Polish, Spanish, Portuguese, it was all mixed. Vailsburg was Irish, most of them. It was a nice clean city, orderly. When the riots came, that was too bad. I think the riots were the downfall of Newark because they all start bailing out then.

F. Grehl: (appointed 1948) It was a marvelous city, probably one of the best in the nation. You had everything and anything you wanted. It was a clean, nice city. We had our minority section down in Springfield Avenue, South Orange Avenue, Broome and Prince Streets, and Howard and in there. There was poverty and squalor in that area. They just stayed there by themselves and didn't bother anybody. It was safe city. My wife and I used to walk on Sundays right down South Orange Avenue to downtown and go to the movies. Sometimes we'd walk home at night. You had everything you wanted in the city from opera to burlesque, four or five great movies. The Adams Theater was where all the great Big Bands would come in. It was close to Irvington which had Olympic Amusement Park. You had everything, excellent transportation. To me it was one of the finest cities around.

During the war, a lot of people came into Newark. Newark was a great manufacturing city. During the war there were people needed in the factories. A lot of people came into Newark and filled the void of all the people away at war. Of course, when you came home the apartments and dwellings were all at a minimum. They were available, but it's a law of supply and demand. There were a lot of people who wanted it. Instead of getting forty dollars a months, they get forty-five or fifty. After all my pay was only seventy-eight dollars twice a month, the first and the fifteenth.

After the war, a lot of people started coming from the south. That's when they started those high-rise projects. When they started building the one right across from Six Engine it was all white people in there. All around Six Engine was mostly Italians, Fairmont Avenue, Hunterdon Street, and so forth. Gradually the people started moving out of the neighborhood. It's like everything else. The great the American dream, they wanted a home in the suburbs and they started doing that. As they vacated, it was basically filled with minorities in the Central Ward. The Italian people moved up to Vailsburg and their void was filled with minorities. They had larger families. It was the same with the school system. The school system started getting over taxed. And little by little we had too much density for the facilities that were available.

You just couldn't live in the city of Newark and send your kids to school there. I had to send my kids to private Catholic school in Irvington, because I lived right on the borderline of Irvington. People couldn't live in Newark and send their kids to private schools. That's when they started moving out and getting housing that was fit for their size family. Except for Vailsburg and those sections, Newark was basically apartment house structures and people didn't want to rent to kids. They didn't want to rent if you had animals. When I first had children, I couldn't get an apartment because I had kids. Nobody would rent to me. That's when people started moving here and there.

Vesey: (appointed 1948) Oh, down neck was down neck, North Newark was pretty residential, pretty stable. All the Jews were over in the South Ward, South Side. Vailsburg was German/Irish. All the colors were mostly in the Central Ward down at Prince Street, Spruce Street down in that area until they started building the projects. It was ethnic neighborhoods more or less. The city was pretty well evened out as far as ethnic breakdowns.

McCormack: (appointed 1949) This was a blue-collar town in my youth. It was a town of factories, industries of all types. There were a lot of blue-collar jobs in this town, huge industries in this town. Bell and Howell telephone and radio was in this town, a major employer. Ronson cigarette lighter was down by Military Park. There were so many of them, Westinghouse, General Electric, huge companies that hired hundreds and hundreds of people. They were blue collar type jobs that were in the shipyard, railroads, the trucking industry, and manufacturing plants. It was an industrial city with jobs all over the place. You had a couple of bastions of wealthy people perhaps or people slightly above the blue-collar class. Like the Forest Hill section was in the early days. In my day it was society hill if you wanted to call it that. There were larger homes up there. You didn't have your crowded three story frames that you had in other neighborhoods. You had large homes, which, in those days, seemed almost like estates. I mean if you had a hundred feet, a hundred and fifty feet lot it seemed like an estate. They had driveways. They had cars, well manicured lawns. A lot of people had domestic help. They had maids, chauffeurs, butlers, and people of that type. They hired gardeners.

When you go up there now and look at those houses they probably seem small by today's standards. You might say the middle class has taken over those homes that were once society homes, but in my youth in Newark that was society hill. Those people up there were wealthy people. There were a lot of lawyers and manufacturing people, people from the business community in Newark. There were no blue-collar people in that area. The other area that was probably a little better off was the Weequahic section, which was heavily Jewish in those days. You had a lot of merchants over there. Probably you had a lot of business people and merchants who had various businesses in Newark. They had nice homes up there, better than the three story frames of the working class.

It was a teeming city in those days. Broad and Market Streets in those days, they used to say it was the busiest corner in the world. Twenty-four hours a day it looked like Times Square. There was a policeman on duty twenty-four hours a day. I remember as a little kid there was a traffic tower, a big tower, right in the middle of the four corners. It was a gothic size structure with the lights on each side and that used to direct traffic. It was right out in the middle of the street. They took that out in the '40s, but that was there in the early days. That was a busy corner.

The city was my home. The only place I ever lived. I was born in the city. I grew up in the city. It was home. All my friends lived here. I went to school here. I went to church here. I think that the city started to change right after World War II. All the veterans were coming back from World War II. There were literally thousands of them. Every family had a couple of sons in the service. Every family, there's nothing similar, Vietnam or any other war, that would match the total number of people involved in World War II. Every single household had someone in the service, a brother or father. It was mostly men in those days, but the point is that when the war ended, these guys started coming back and getting married. There was a deluge of guys looking for houses.

The families that these guys left when they got drafted were living in these three story frames in Newark, in four or five room apartments with their parents, brothers, and sisters. When they came back, they'd get married and very often had to move back into those same apartments. They'd have a room as a married couple with his parents or her parents. There was no construction. There was no housing in Newark. The existing housing was what was there and it was solidly occupied. Nobody was selling houses. There was a tremendous demand for housing for these young veterans. They were getting married. They were starting families and they needed housing.

I remember too, because I myself experienced this. In those days if you wanted to buy a house in the city of Newark because the buildings were old, we were told you had to come up with a twenty percent down payment. That was mandated if you wanted to get a mortgage, a twenty percent down payment. The average house in Newark in those days might have been selling for ten thousand dollars. So a twenty percent down payment was only two thousand dollars, but two thousand dollars was an astronomical amount of money in those days. Very few guys had that kind of money.

When I came on the job as a new fireman, I made twenty-four hundred dollars a year. There weren't any two-income families. Most of the girls, when you married, left work and stayed home to become housewives. So we were living on twenty-four hundred dollars a year. Trying to pay rent, have a car if you had a car, and save money. It was pretty hard. These people were desperate. They couldn't find housing. Then these developers came in and started buying up land outside the perimeter of Newark. In Union, in Clark, in Rahway, which were close by. You could buy a house, a tract house. If you were a veteran, they had signs all over the place. "Veterans, No Down Payment." You could buy a house out there if you had a steady job like a fireman. Walk out, look at a house, sign a paper, and move into the house the next day. All these young veterans and their wives were bailing out to get a place to live.

The other thing that sped this whole process up and made it feasible was the advent of the Garden State Parkway and the New Jersey Turnpike. You could jump on the Parkway up in East Orange and be down in Clark or Rahway in ten or fifteen minutes. It was no worse than a commute from Vailsburg to down neck, if you lived in Vailsburg and had to go down neck. There were hundreds of houses going up in these little suburbs. You could walk in and if you had twenty bucks in your pocket to pay the closing cost, you could move in the next morning. That's exactly what guys did. That's where the exodus came from. People started moving out.

A lot of people honestly tried to stay in the city at the time because the city was home to them. But they couldn't find a house to buy. There were few houses available because Newark was a very stable community. If you did find a house, they'd tell you to come up with twenty percent down and these young kids didn't have that kind of money. So, they bailed out. That's what started the snowballing effect. I'd say that started right after World War II, in the late '40s and the early '50s. It continued right up into the '60s and then it really snowballed. Faster and faster, as if the snowball were rolling down the mountain and picking up speed. But in the beginning it was because there was no available housing in the city. You couldn't buy a house at any price.

Masterson: (appointed 1949) I was born and raised in Newark. It was beautiful. If Newark was like that today, I never would have left it. When I was growing up, it was beautiful. The neighborhoods were good. The people were good. You could walk anywhere. The streets were safe. It was a really nice city. You had downtown Newark. They used to come from way out, all the suburbs, come shopping downtown Newark. They had about four or five theaters down there. They were all good. They had a few decent restaurants. I wasn't interested in it, but they had the wrestling over there on Eighteenth Avenue, bicycle racing up in Vailsburg, and the boxing arena with outdoor fights up there across from Vailsburg Park. They had the skating rink. They used to have the Newark Bears. We used to get the knot hole tickets to see the Newark games. You'd get them for nothing almost. The only thing you had to worry about, get a sandwich and ten cents, a nickel down a nickel back on the trolley. You'd be all the way down neck. We'd spend the second nickel down there and we'd walk home from way down neck. I lived up in the Roseville section, up by Saint Rose of Lima's.

The city was Irish, Italian, I guess mostly. I was growing up with Irish, Italian mostly, but Newark had everything. They had Germans over there around Springfield Avenue. There were some nice Italian neighborhoods at Fourteenth Avenue, over in that area and down the ward, Eighth Avenue,

Clifton Avenue. Down neck you had a lot of Polish. The beautiful part of it was, whatever you wanted to eat, you could just go to those neighborhoods. You could buy from your Polish butcher, your German butcher, your Italian butcher. If you wanted a leg of veal, you'd go to an Italian butcher. If you wanted sausage and knockwurst, you go to a German butcher like A.M. Teller. Everything was first class. In fact there were places that had home made liverwurst right on the avenue. It really was a beautiful city.

Baldino: (appointed 1951) The city had been divided into several ethnic enclaves only because most of the people came from all parts of the world to live near relatives. We had sections of the city that were predominantly Italian, the North Ward, Irish and German, the West Ward, Jewish, the South Ward, Polish, the East Ward, and Afro-American, the Central Ward. Each ward had a combination of all the groups.

Deutch: (appointed 1953) The city was a very strong city. It was probably seventy five per cent white in those days as far as race. Eighteen months after I got on the job, I transferred to Five Truck and there were a lot of white people up on Belmont Avenue all around us. Even on Belmont and Waverly, we had a lot of white neighbors. There was one colored fireman on the job when I came on. He was Willie Thomas and I think he came on in 1951 or '52.

Griffith: (appointed 1953) When I was a young guy it was broken up into areas. North Newark it was a high Italian population. Then out in the Forest Hill area there was a mixture of Irish, English, and maybe some German people along with Italians. The Ironbound had a little bit of everybody. The Central Ward had a lot of black families. South Ward was heavily Jewish and of course the West Ward was heavily Irish with civil service workers.

It was working class. I was born and brought up in the North Ward area, in Roseville area around the city stadium. In that area most of the people were either teachers or worked for the city. It was a good place to live. North Newark especially was nice. The city itself was nice. I think one of the big things is that most of the people who worked for the fire department lived in Newark. The Police lived in Newark. The teachers lived in Newark. Everybody who worked here lived here. And that made it even nicer. To me it was a super place to be brought up in at that time.

Wall: (appointed 1954) Nice. Newark was ethnic then. If you were Irish you went to either Saint James or Saint Colmba parish. If you were Polish, you went to Saint Casmir's. The Italians, I guess Mount Carmel, but we all sort of intermixed socially. And of course, the guys intermixed by having fistfights in the local parks occasionally. I don't remember anyone getting more than a black eye out of it. Newark was an interesting place.

Newark at that time was almost four hundred thousand. Because when I came on the job even in '54, we were something like three hundred and eighty thousand. We were far larger than Jersey City and now Jersey City population wise has almost the same numbers as Newark because they weren't as devastated as we were.

Freeman: (appointed 1956) Oh, it was great. I was born in the city and lived in the city. At that time it was good. It was the hub of everything. You had the airport, Penn Station, a railroad, buses, the downtown area. Prince Street you had all the push carts, all the Jewish stores there. You could buy anything you wanted on Springfield Avenue. You could walk there and walk back. It was a real safe city.

I grew up on Somerset Street. My family is from Clinton. That's where my mother was born, Clinton, New Jersey. They came in to Newark. They lived in North Newark, Delavan Avenue and then they moved right off Broad Street. They lived down there until finally they moved into the Prudential Apartments on Somerset Street. I was born there. My grandmother moved to number one, which is on the corner of Montgomery Street. The Prudential apartments were beautiful then. We had tennis courts in the back. They had a playground for the kids. That was between Spruce and Montgomery. The apartments belonged to Prudential, but the grounds belonged to the city and they still belong to the city today. In the summertime they put a sprinkler out in the middle of the area. They had benches, grass, and flowers. It was really, really, beautiful. We had no problems there.

Then I moved to Belmont Avenue in the spring of 1942, after the war started because the family started to expand. There were four of us down there in I think it was one bedroom. We had to move. We didn't have any room. We moved to Belmont Avenue, which was over the top of a roofing place called Rothman and Cohen. It was three bedrooms upstairs with a big dining room, a big living room, and a big kitchen, nice place. It was one family on the second floor and the business on the ground floor. We lived there many years. I'd say into the early '60s maybe. Then they moved us to East Orange to my sister's house.

I remember when we first moved there. The place was infested with mice and roaches. The guy had rented out the different rooms. I mean mice all over the place. We put traps down. I remember this paste that used to glow in the dark. Called Jay-o paste, I think that was the name of it. You put it on slices of potatoes. You'd stick it along the walls, under the sink, on top of the counter. You'd go into the kitchen, turn the lights on, and there'd be roaches all over the place. We fought that for a long, long time, the roaches and the mice. But the good thing about it was we were by ourselves. We had nobody else to contend with because it was just a one family house on the second floor. Twenty-one steps up and on Saturdays somebody had to wash those steps down all the way down and do the hallway and the vestibule. The vestibule was tile and tile floor.

There were nine of us: six girls and three boys. My father was the only one who worked. He worked at Singer Sewing Machine Company in Elizabeth, Elizabeth Port. So we had a pretty good existence. Everything was in walking distance. Prince Street, the Jews owned almost everything in the neighborhood. In fact the store next to the firehouse across the street, Izzy's we used to call it, we used to go right next door to the firehouse and get meats. Then on the other side of the firehouse was Belmont Liquors, which was Gershenbaum's. If that's not Jewish, his mother's name was Bella and his father's name was Sam.

In most of the stores, even down where I lived on Somerset Street, they had three by five cards. You could get a loaf of bread, a quart of milk, or whatever. If you didn't have the money, he'd write it on a little card and he'd put the amount after it. He'd put it in a little file box. On payday when you came in, you'd ask him, "How much do I owe you?" And you'd give him the money. Everything was above board. Everything was honest.

We had no problems racially that I ever knew of. In the South it was rampant. They were hanging blacks. They called them niggers then, that whole nine yards down South. They tell me it was hidden in the north, but it was there. But in that neighborhood I don't remember any. Maybe it was because I was young. I didn't know it. You're talking Spruce Street,

Somerset, Quitman, Montgomery Street, Kinney Street, Prince Street. All up Spruce Street, all the way up to Belmont Avenue, High Street, Quitman those were all our streets, Quitman, Prince, Charlton, although I didn't go above there because we couldn't. Monmouth Street School was right across the street from where I lived on Somerset Street. We lived at forty-seven, fifth floor walk up.

I went to Monmouth Street School. There was a little candy store right next door to school where everybody would go in the morning. You'd pick up your candy. A loaf of bread was twenty-five cents; a quart of milk was a quarter. You could buy cigarettes for a penny a piece. He broke open a pack of cigarettes if you didn't have the money. Give me two cigarettes. And if you didn't have the money, the guy would put it on a little three by five card and fill it in. You'd pay at the end of the week or whenever payday was. There was never any problem. So, it was a good neighborhood. We played ball there when we were kids, in the back. There was a kid, Holomon Jarmel. He was a little short, fat Jewish kid. We'd all play baseball together. I went to school with a kid named Milton Schilfer and they named a park after his brother, Schilfer Park. There's a little memorial right there in the middle of the park. His brother was one of the guys killed in the war in I think Pearl Harbor.

I don't remember too many fires. Maybe I was too young to realize a lot of things. But it was a great city. You could walk all over the place. We'd walk down town. You name the way. Usually we walked over to Springfield Avenue and then walked down to Market Street. Bamberger's was the big store then and it was very busy. Broad and Market Street was a historical business center at that time. It was one of the biggest business centers, I guess in the state at that particular time. If you look at pictures you see trolleys and all kinds of stuff down there. We'd walk all the way down Broad Street, up Spruce Street, up Kinney Street. Those are hills. Or we'd walk across High Street, which was easier, and home.

At night, we'd be out until eight thirty playing kick the can, catch one catch all, hide and go seek. It was a great, great living. There was harmony. You had kid's fights, but nothing beyond that. You had all the Jewish stores in the neighborhood. You could go anywhere and they'd grind the meat up for you. Up on Prince Street, they had live chickens or turkeys. Right on the corner, there was a place right on the corner of Charlton and Spruce. Then there was a good vegetable store between Prince and Charlton called Southern Produce. They had all this stuff. It'd come out half way to the sidewalk. It was all the produce. I mean, you name it and you can get it there, really, really good stuff. Everybody would stop in there.

Shoes, there was a shoe store on the corner of Prince and Spruce. There was Lipschicht's, which was a deli right on the south west corner of Prince Street. There was sawdust on the floor. I think they had brass rails in there. There was another deli on Prince Street, a lot of delis around. Springfield Avenue right there just below Charlton Street or Beacon Street, there was another deli there. You could get a four or five inch sandwich, roast beef, corned beef, whatever. Army and Navy store right there on Spruce Street, I used to go in there and buy fatigues. The girl, their daughter, and I became good friends. She worked in a nursery where my daughter used to go. I'd go in that store all the time and buy fatigues because I couldn't afford a suit or shirts or anything like that. You had every thing there. Whatever you wanted was within walking distance, a loaf of bread, clothing, whatever. And if you wanted a suit or a hat, Springfield Avenue, you had shops like that on Springfield Avenue, too. It was just a good city. Bamberger's was the big store and Haynes.

I remember parades in the city, really good parades. Many, many years ago I remember the Thanksgiving Day parade would come down West Market Street and end at Bamberger's. Santa Claus would get off at Bamberger's. They would have that Halsey and Market Bamberger's window there. That would be beautiful. They would have all the mechanized Christmas things in that window, the dolls, the elves, the Santa Clauses, and the trains. If you were meeting somebody down there, "Well, where can we meet?" "Well, maybe under the clock in Bamberger's." That was the place where you would always meet people. The stores down town were beautiful. You had plenty of places to go, plenty of places to shop. You didn't have crime down there then.

Now in the other parts of the city, going out towards the north, you had all the Italians. In fact, down neck was Italian, too. Before the Portuguese came in, there were Italians down neck. And over in the Weequahic section they were Jewish. All the Jewish people were there, all up, up going towards Irvington, going out towards Lyons Avenue, Chancellor Avenue, all over in that area. I would image all along Elizabeth Avenue, they had the big apartment buildings. I guess in North Newark that Italian section came all the way down through Broadway, all the way out to Belleville. I know Belleville was Italian, so I would image that was pretty close. You had plenty of buses. Transportation was great. I can remember trolleys going back to when I was a kid, the Five Kinney with the poles and the wires. That was fantastic. So, it was a good life.

You couldn't do anything wrong with out somebody knowing about it. Your neighbor, your neighbor's kid, your mother's friends and by the time you got home, if you did something wrong, your mother would know. You didn't have to have a telephone. We didn't have a telephone for a long time. My mother didn't work, but if she wasn't home, by the time she got home when you were doing something wrong. You got it. "So and so told me you did so and so. Did you do it? And don't lie. Don't lie." You had respect for your parents. You had respect for adults, no matter who they were or what they where. You know the Bible said, "Don't spare the rod." The rod was not spared in a lot of households there. I would say at that particular period of time at our age, everybody was pretty much on about the same level of discipline. You couldn't stay out beyond say eight thirty because when it got dark, in the house. If you didn't, then your parent would come down stairs with a belt and you'd get whipped up stairs or spanked up stairs. I remember my mother spanked me up Spruce Street one day, when we moved and I went down to play. I didn't come home when I should have, right up Spruce Street boy, bang, bang, every block. "And don't you run either. If you run I'm going to get you." Oh, how embarrassing that was. That was embarrassing. Your mother's walking behind you with a belt. "Come back here."

In the evening, when you came home from school and went out to play, we usually played stickball. They didn't call it stickball, then, but it was. You had a little stick and we had a tennis ball. We played baseball that way. The father of this guy Chubby used to come home from work I guess around five o'clock. He'd stick his head out a back window whistle. Everybody heard that and half the gang would go because your mother told you, "When Chubby's father tells him to come upstairs or whistles you come up stairs, too." That broke the game up. If I didn't come upstairs, my mother would yell out the window, "Come upstairs right now. What's the matter? You can't hear me? You hard of hearing? Wait until you get upstairs?" Now you have to expect a spanking when you got upstairs.

We didn't go across the street. You had to ask to go across the street. A lot of kids went across the street. We had the playground there,

Monmouth Street School. The playground was there and in the evening they showed movies in the playground. You'd sit down on the bench and they'd have the little corrugated cover over the roof, protecting you if it rained. We'd see movies in the evening and we'd play checkers. Basketball a little bit, it wasn't as prevalent then as it is now. The girls would jump rope, the whole nine yards in the playground there. It was good. Then you would come home after the playground. They had recreation right after school. They would open up. They'd bring out all the checkers and chess and all the games, all kinds of tittely winks and all kinds of other things. You had some place to go, something to do. School was good. If you did something wrong in school, you'd get it. You'd better go to school. I think I played hooky from school one time and almost got caught. That's because my cousins were a little less disciplined than I was. My aunt worked, so they more or less did what they wanted to do and they kind of went by the way side. I don't think either one of them finished high school at all. I wish those times would come back. .

There were fights between Italians and blacks because they crossed the line. They went across town, especially over around Orange Street, in that area. I think over there, there was always something going on between the Italians and the blacks. There were a lot of skirmishes between blacks and Italians, and also in the school system over that way. Not much where I lived. That was amongst ourselves, because it was one big area, the Third Ward, and not many Italians came over this way. We never had a problem with the Jews.

McGee: (appointed 1956) Well, I was born where the old city hospital was on Fairmount Avenue. I'm from that area for most of my life. I moved to East Orange at about maybe seven years of age or so. I went to school in

East Orange and then went to Sacred Heart, which is in Vailsburg. I went to Saint James High School down neck in Newark. Went in the Army and then came on the job. The city was great growing up as a kid because it was neighborhoods. We're talking about ethnic neighborhoods. Vailsburg was known to be Irish and Italian. Down neck was known to be Italian and Polish. The South Ward was known to be mostly Jewish, the North Ward mostly Italian. And the Central Ward even back in those days was predominantly black. In fact, Camden Street, which was just a block above Bergen Street, was black when I was an infant. There were a lot more white people in the City, but they were still divided ethnically in their own groups for the most part. But no major problems, it was a great place to grow up and it was a great place to raise a family I'm sure for other people. A good city, I still like it.

McGrory: (appointed 1957) It was a workingman's city with quite a bit of diversified industry. The problem with Newark was it was very small. In land area, what's it twenty-one, twenty three square miles. Twenty-three square miles, that's not much when you talk about a city with four hundred and ten thousand people in it. And then if you look at a map and see how much of that area is devoted to a port area and an airport area, there's not a lot of room for four hundred and ten thousand people to live. It was the mostly densely populated city in the country. The city was a workingman's city, not enough area to expand. My dad, who came to this country from Scotland in 1907, lived on Mount Prospect Avenue. Some of the rich people of the city were living up on Mount Prospect Avenue. They were moving out right after the turn of the century because there was no place for the upper class to live. They were going to South Orange whatever.

That's probably a big part of what happened in Newark. There was no breathing area for anything to happen. There was so much industry, so many three story frames. Vailsburg was a little bit different. North Newark was a little bit different, but the real affluent people moved out of the city. I liked the city. I was born in Newark in a hospital, but my family lived in Kearny, in Harrison, East Newark. In January of '42 we moved over to Newark. So I finished up grammar school in Holy Cross, Harrison. Then I went to West Side High School and after that I went to work.

Downtown Newark had great movie theaters, Loews, Proctors, The Paramount, The Bradford. Big names used to come to the Adams Theater on Bradford Place when I was younger. Big stores, good stores like Bamberger's which everyone seems to think of as a department store, but they had a meat market in there that was tops. They had restaurants downtown. Kresge's was another good department store. Hayne's was a top-flight department store. You had Military Park there. All the small parks in downtown Newark were beautiful. Some of the nicest statue work you could see is in the parks downtown. The river was always bad because industry lined up on that river. When I was a kid, you could just about walk across.

I liked the city. My memories of Newark in my young teens during World War II are of a really vibrant city. We had quite an influx of people from other states, mainly from Pennsylvania. So, there's another mix that we had, then in the '50s or maybe even before that, the Portuguese started coming in. It was different. There were always different people coming in. The city of Newark always had a diverse population. In the Weequahic section, there were quite a few Jewish people. There were Germans, but the Germans moved up to Irvington early on. Italians, Irish, Polish, everyone came in. There were always blacks in Newark in certain areas. After the first war, my father said, there was a big influx of blacks who came into the area. Then after the second war the same thing happened. After that the Puerto Ricans came in the '50s.

Denvir: (appointed 1959) It was a nice city at the time. I was born and raised in Newark. I was living in Vailsburg on Smith Street when I came on the job. Vailsburg was mainly white. Maybe there were some blacks in the projects, a few homes scattered through, but when I came on it was mostly white.

Freda: (appointed 1959) When I first was appointed to the fire department in 1959, I was stationed in a fire house that was opposite the corner I grew up hanging on, the corner across the street from Fifteen Engine. As kids making devious plans I would play some jokes on the firemen across the street. In fact, one of the firemen in that firehouse when I was hanging on the corner as a kid is a Deputy Chief. I remember him. He went on up the ranks and he's a chief. He's still on the job today. So, when I feel old, I just think how he feels.

But the city was a very stable city then. The Park Avenue firehouse was the type of firehouse that you would sit outside on the old wooden captain's chairs. They'd be lined up in the summer right across both bays and people would stop and talk to you. People would come into the firehouse. The neighbors and the firemen got along very well. It was unheard of for someone to break into a firehouse and steal anything. In fact, we didn't shut doors to firehouses then. The neighbors would come out and shut the doors.

There was a candy store next door run by a women. We would literally go in there, sit there, and talk to the woman and she'd be forcing you to eat lunch with her. It was close enough where if the bell rang you could run next door, a very friendly, stable atmosphere. Crime, crime wasn't a big deal then at all. It was unheard of to have a fireman's car broken into. I can't remember an instance of a firehouse being broken into or anything taken or any problem at a fire with the civilians. Believe it or not, when I went over to Twelve Engine the same thing existed. Most of the firefighters there were white. We were in a totally black community. It was very neighbor conscious. We used to sit outside. Again, the neighbors were very close, right in the middle of the ghetto. While I was there, my car was never bothered. The house was never broken into. Nothing was ever taken.

I think the big change came about when the influx of narcotics hit. That's what caused all the problems with the crime around the firehouses; how the city became destabilized; and where the crime rate went up. The other factor was a lot of firemen had moved out of Newark already, but I saw no reason to move out. I was very happy living in Newark, had a family in Newark. My wife could walk out on Roseville Avenue at night. Newark had a very good school system. The big thing then was if you lived in Vailsburg. If a fireman or policeman was really doing well, he bought a house in Vailsburg. That was the ultimate. You really admired people who did that.

At the time I came on the job, Newark was predominantly white. I don't know the percentages, but North Newark was all white. The area I lived in was all Italian. Around the Sixteenth, Seventeenth Avenue area, that area was all Italian. The other predominant group would be blacks and they seemed to be located in the Central Ward. There was segregation in those days, very strong. Black people didn't come into your area and you didn't go into their area as civilians. Nobody seemed to really mind it or beef about it. But in essence the black people were trapped in the ghetto. That was a very poor area.

The area around Fifteen Engine when I was a kid and up to my early time on the fire department was broken down into ethnic enclaves where there was no such thing as integration as far as the city goes. There was an Irish area. South of Park Avenue was predominantly all Irish, North Sixth Street, North Seventh Street, and so forth. Go north of Park Avenue, going north on the same street, South Sixth Street, was predominantly Italian. There weren't too many mixes. There were slight exceptions were you'd have an Irish family living amongst the Italians and vise a versa. In fact there was a black family on Sixth Street, which was like a historical billing. Now this was when I was a kid, but I still remember the woman, Mrs. Washington was her name. Even in those days, she was a highly respected woman because people would draw a difference. They would say she's a nice black person. Her kids went to college and she works hard and they would throw away those stereotypes.

But I remember distinctly as a small child, the Italian immigrants, like my friends' fathers and mothers didn't even speak English. We're talking about people out of Ellis Island. They were uptight. Italians in that era were all funny. They strictly wanted to be about their own kind. There wasn't intermarriage between even the ethnics. But surprising enough, they used to speak very highly often about Mrs. Washington because if you were sick, she would always be at your house. Unheard of for a black person to come to your house in those days, but she would be welcomed into your house. She'd always bring you fruit and juice if she heard you were sick or something. It was very unusual. Like today, you might not think much about it, but that was a conversation piece, that this black person lived on

North Sixth Street and was accepted. It was something to talk about. That's why I remember her name. It was a unique thing in those days.

So, what I was trying to express. You had the Italian neighborhood. You had the Irish neighborhoods and the black people, in my early fire department experience, were mostly in the Central Ward. Then they started to spread out in the city more. As the white people retreated from the city, more and more blacks move in and spread out. You had the Jewish section. The Weequahic section was block after block after block of strictly Jewish families. That's the way it was. If you were in a firehouse in those areas, I certainly think it would affect your thinking and operations because you would be part of that social and economic area.

Charpentier: (appointed 1959) The city was pretty good at that time. We were busy, but the attitude of the people toward the fire department was a lot different than in later years. I mean, before we were the heroes. We got along whether it was black, white, purple, or green, male, female. We got along with all the people. I would say the city was about eighty per cent white and twenty per cent black. The black people were in their own area, which was the Central Ward. Blacks were just starting to move into the Weequahic section, but that was still ninety percent Jewish. You had Vailsburg. That was ninety-nine percent white. North Newark was mostly white, Italians. Down neck, well, that was almost a hundred percent white.

Marcell: (appointed 1959) When I first went on up to Eleven Engine it was a really, really nice place up there. The Presbyterian Hospital was there. The Sisters of the Poor were there. The neighborhood was really nice. It gradually, gradually got worse. I think when I went there they went out about three hundred and twenty times a year, Eleven Engine. I think the truck went out about two hundred and fifty times, but as the years went on things got really bad.

Smith: (appointed 1959) The majority of the city was white. You had enclaves of blacks and down along South Broad Street going in a few blocks, you had Hispanics. There were a lot of wood frame buildings all over the city. The projects on Waverly Avenue, Prince Street in that area, they weren't completed yet. There were still on the side streets going off it, it was all wood frame. In fact, the majority of the city was wood frame.

Miller: (appointed 1959) I always lived in the city. I was born in Newark. I lived on Twelve Cabinet Street right next to the rectory for nineteen years until I got married. I got married at Saint James church down neck and I lived down neck for about a year. Then I lived in North Newark at twenty-one Halleck Street, where I was appointed to the job, after that I moved to five oh one Hawthorne Avenue.

At the time the city was a very industrious city. It was a very busy, hustling city. Downtown Newark, I think was one of the four busiest corners in the world for populace. At the time I think we had almost four hundred thousand people in the city of Newark. There were over a hundred theaters and dozens of churches and synagogues. I was told there were a hundred and thirty five theaters in Newark. It was possible because every neighborhood had two or three theaters. That's why the fire department had such a big theater detail.

There were many restaurants to go to, many Jewish Deli's, German Jewish restaurants on Prince Street, where you got good corned beef. You had Stosh's. My impression was it was a very hard working, very well mixed ethnically wise group of people. You had the German, the Irish, and

Italians in various sections of the city. The First Ward was mostly Italians, around Seventh Avenue. That section, even when you were young, you couldn't go in there if you looked Irish. They would question you. Maybe beat you up and tell you to get out of the neighborhood. The black populace was mostly around West Market Street, Boston, in that area. Vailsburg was German Irish, the North Ward was Italian, and the Weequahic section was predominantly Jewish. It was a very cohesive society. Everybody stuck together.

I started playing baseball in semi-pro because I had had some good tutorage. I was playing with the guy who just was inducted into the Hall of Fame. He was a black baseball player, lived on Boston Street right on the corner from me. I didn't know that in his youth he played in all the black leagues. He played third base. I forget what his name was, but we as a white team used to play them down Newark Bear Stadium. Being with people like that, you learned a lot. You learned how to play baseball properly. No little leagues. We didn't have that. We just had sandlot ball, but I was fortunate enough to get into this with some people who were ex major leaguers. So at the time I was sixteen years old I was playing with people who had been in the major leagues. Semi-pro ball up in the Essex County League. Maybe they played fifty or sixty games a year plus maybe three or four in other leagues during the week. The old West Side League which in West Side Park. They had lights. We played night games there. You'd get about four or five hundred people and they'd pass the hat around. That paid for that. But Newark was a good city to live in at the time.

You could get beat up because I did a couple of times. Got chased out, but in the area where the blacks were there was not too much racial tension. Although when I was about thirteen years old there was a big war in the park over on Orange Street near Branch Brook Park. The blacks and Italians had a big fight. I mean this involved thousands of people with baseball bats and everything. I don't know if it ever made the news or what ever at that time. The news media wasn't around, but it was a tremendous battle. There was a different type of intolerance, not hatred, but it was territorial.

I can recall, I was sixteen years old and I was dating this girl who lived up on South Eighteenth Street. I had to walk from Cabinet Street, over Norfolk Street, and take the Thirty One South Orange up to her home. Coming home one evening around ten o'clock I had to walk past the old Robert Treat Grammar School which was situated on I think Fourteenth Avenue and Norfolk Street. Across the street there was a black club. I'll never forget because I was walking by and the guys yelled over, "Hey, man. Hey, Zeke. Your name Zeke?" I said, "No, my name is not Zeke." It was half a block, not even half a block away, from one corner to the other.

The next thing you know I was getting beat up by about ten blacks. Really getting beat up. It was comical because they really weren't hitting me. They were getting shots in, but there were so many of them that they were hitting themselves. It was like a Three Stooges comedy. While they were all converging on me, somehow I got out through the middle underneath and I could run like hell. I ran away. They couldn't catch me. But there were at least ten of them. They were older, maybe in their twenties, some in their thirties. They were drinking. They were not fleet of foot, so they couldn't catch me. When I got home I did have a couple teeth that were really loose. Eventually I lost the teeth in the front. That's the only problem I had with blacks growing up with them because there were some in the neighborhood. There was a black doctor I knew. Black kids whose parents were doctors in Saint Joseph's school. There was no really racial tension like we have today. It was a different type of tension, just territorial. Sometimes they got mad if you went into their territory.

The Weequahic section was predominantly Jewish and they stuck to their own. They controlled the wealth of the city probably at that time. They had all the big businesses over there. They just stayed amongst themselves. There were no problems with any kind of race wars with those. And in the school system in the Central Ward, was seventy thirty as far as the mixture because that was where they mostly congested in the Central Ward. There was no Spanish. There were a few Gypsies living around the area in storefronts. In my school there were maybe five per cent black. There were never any problems with race.

You didn't belong in the Italian section if you were Irish. I was Irish and German, so I stayed around Hudson and West Market Street, around Saint Joe's. Everybody stayed in their own territory. We went to our own movies, the Dento Theater, the Core Theater, the Essex, or the Plaza. We never went over to North Newark where the other movies were. They had gangs, the Turo's and the Lucky Elevens. They were all in the First Ward. If you were in their movie, you'd better have one of their jackets on or something like that. You couldn't go in their territory. They just didn't appreciate it. Like the Weequahic Dire, people went there. You could go there. There was no problem, but if you went over to some of the theaters on Broadway near Halleck Street and you weren't from the neighborhood, you could have some problems over there. They'd punch you around and things like that. I heard stories like that, but you'd have to be looking for trouble too or they'd be looking for trouble. And there was always somebody looking for trouble, but I stayed out of it. I was mostly interested in sports, so I didn't get involved in any of that stuff.

Dunn: (appointed 1959) I was born and raised in the East Ward of Newark and I went to a Catholic parochial school. I think the perception I had of the city was limited because at that time you didn't travel out of your community that much. I lived on a street that was all white and either Irish, German, or Italian. There were a few Polish people and that was your nationality mix. Everybody had gone to Catholic school and your friends were confined more or less to the people who you went to school with who lived on the street. Two blocks away from us was a low cost housing project. That was also 99 point 9 percent white at the time. That was due to the fact that after World War II or during the war people were brought in from Pennsylvania to work in our factories and they lived in these types of dwellings. They again were the same nationality and racial mix as the Catholic school. Most of them went to Catholic school. We had a very vibrant Catholic school of really three or four nationalities of people. Basically poor, but we just didn't realize it. That's why we lived on the third floor in a house. I thought we lived on the third floor because you get a better view. That's because that's the way your education went. You were brought up to be optimistic about things. That certainly has changed my outlook on life as I go through it.

The city at that time in the East Ward was doing fine. There was really no problem. I lived right at the street where Ballantine Brewery was; it employed thousands of people. So, you knew about work; everybody went to work. Everybody's father or family member worked in this major employer. Public Service was a prestigious job. New Jersey Bell was a prestige job. And working in the paint companies on the island was a very prestigious job at the time. Because they had all amassed what I considered a substantial amount of money after the war. If you work and you don't spend your money; you save money. So everybody had money, everybody had cars. The downtown area of Newark where you went was a vibrant area. We had Bamberger's Department Store, which was our large department store. I never went down to Hayne's Department Store because that was where the rich people went. I went to Ohrbach's.

There were several movies. I remember at different times going on the bus to downtown Newark to the movies with my family. One of the vivid memories I have is of the Adams Theater, which always had a stage show, of seeing the Three Stooges live as a kid. Then as you grow older, seeing them on TV, they were just as funny then fooling around on the stage in Newark.

We used to once in a while take the Thirty-one bus to Maplewood. As you went from downtown to the Maplewood line you would be going to housing that you just didn't see if you were down neck. It seemed if you were going to work and be successful the idea would be to live in a one family house with a driveway, which just didn't exist down neck. I always thought that's where the rich people lived. I knew a fireman as a kid who was very community oriented. His name was Harp Bacon. He lived on 11th Street and South Orange Avenue and he used to bring the kids to his house for Christmas, as we do today, only under different racial things and different ideas. But he did the same thing. He took children out of the three story frame and brought them up to his house and entertained them over Christmas week. He had a large army of lead soldiers under his Christmas tree. He also had a white Christmas tree which was sprayed with like white wash that I had never seen down neck. He was also like our community relations man in the firehouse down there. He would tow cars away and open hydrants for the kids. The quandary that I have, as I grow older, with a man like that was: Why he lived up there and spent his whole social life in a different section of the city. I never knew he had a family and yet his son was a Newark fireman. So his whole social life revolved around the Ironbound, but his whole family life was in a whole different section of the city of Newark which I wondered about numerous times as I went through. You know, why did we stay down neck?

At that time there was tremendous peer pressure to climb the mountain. We're still doing the same thing, trying to get out of the city environment and "Do you want to live somewhere?" Then you sit down and you sit home at night and you say, "What am I doing here?"

The other growth factor that I've seen in the city that I remember was when I was young we used to go down to Port Newark all the time. Other guys would take a ride down the shore, whatever you did with your date, we used to take a ride to Port Newark. We would sit on the dock at Port Newark and watch them unload the ships and fantasize about where the ships came from. Because, again very limited experience of getting out of down neck at the time. We really were very close to staying in our little two mile radius of houses. The airport was another favorite stop. You didn't have anything to do, you'd go over to Newark Airport and watch all the rich people get on their airplanes and take a trip. You'd say "Wow that must be great. Imagine going to Pittsburgh on an airplane." So, you looked at that and that's fairly early in life, but all of that has changed. The seaport is now a world-renowned seaport operation. Where there were a few tin huts down there then, now there are a multitude. There are more cars sitting in Port Newark today than probably are in some states in the country; waiting to be shipped out. That stuff didn't exist at that time.

I also remember getting on Route 1 & 9 to go down to Kingsburg and Seabright on Sunday for a shore day and sitting in traffic from Route 1 & 9 in Newark. That's changed. The mobility of the city has changed. People can go anywhere, there's more movement through the city. People down neck have friends in North Newark. People in the South Ward have friends in the West Ward. Really, when I was growing up that just didn't exist. We really stayed in our own area. Most people didn't have cars either, because I lived in an area where you couldn't park your car.

Belzger: (appointed 1959) I was born in the Beth Israel Hospital, 1933. I was a dollar down and a dollar per week type. My father had to pay the clinic costs over years. He used to pay Beth Israel a dollar a month or something like that for years after I was born. He wasn't in the fire department at that time. We lived on Leslie Street, off Hawthorne Avenue. Later on, I grew up on Madison Avenue, right across from Madison Junior High School. And then we lost the house. You could have bought the house for two thousand dollars when I was a kid. Can you image? We lost that and we moved to a cold water flat on Nineteen Avenue and Twentieth Street. We lived there for quite some time. Then, I got married and we still lived there for a while.

My grandfather used to work in Irvington Varnish. He was a gold seal engineer. Irvington Varnish was the fore runner of the 3M company. His name was Gorm Clearwater and he used to make the astounding salary of eighteen dollars a week. That's what we all lived on. My father worked for a company called Farm Crest before he went in the fire department. Farm Crest was on Peddie Street in Newark. It used to be a small bakery. He used to run a small bakery truck for them. But it was a part time job. My dad was a baker. He used to bake apple pies down in Five Truck that rose four inches high. Everybody wanted them. He devised the first small pies when he was in the firehouse later and he sold it to Drakes for a hundred dollars. Drakes took over Farm Crest and all their stops.

Newark to me was Madison Avenue. The neighborhood was fine. It was I guess mostly Irish and German. I never did well in school. I should have, but I was a wise guy. You could walk on the streets of Newark without any problems. The only gangs were us young kids who used to hang around Madison Avenue School or used to be playing play in the yard of Madison. We used to climb the big fence and could play basketball in the wintertime. A lot of people were just hard working people. They didn't have very much. My biggest meal because of my grandfather was a bowl of Wheaties in the morning. Once in a while we'd come into a few dollars and I'd be able to have a sandwich or something like that. It was tough times. I'm not kidding you.

I had the same doctor. His name was Issaic Irwin Miller, for fifty years. He brought me into the world. I can get emotional because he was a wonderful man. I never knew until he died that he was a Medal of Honor holder. He was a major and he was the first doctor into Auschwitz. My wife used to go to his office with the baby carriage, carry the kids in. He'd give them the shots, give them a full physical, give them cookies and milk and charge us fifty cents a piece. Can you imagine? When I lived on Alexander Street I didn't have much money. He knew it. My house cost me fourteen thousand dollars and everything I had went into the house and four kids. He used to apologize later on when the kids were a little bit older; he used to charge us seven dollars for a house call. He thought that was a lot of money. He said he had to do it. But I remember the second time he came back because my kids had high fevers; he didn't charge us anything anyway. That's the kind of man he was. That's the kind of people they were. We used to deal with the butcher and the candy store. I can remember walking to the stores and the people would give you a little piece of candy or anything extra when you bought a loaf of bread. I lived in that neighborhood until I was nine or ten years old and then we went over to Nineteenth Avenue.

Nineteenth Avenue was the same way. It was a three family house, a cold water flat, but the people were generous. I remember my wife and I were married about seven or eight months. It was February. We were in bed one morning and she shakes me. I said, "What's going on?" She said, "It's snowing in here." I said, "So, what?" I was used to it. The houses never were put together too well. We were in the dining room, but we were using it as our bedroom. Five minutes later she shakes me again. She says, "The snow's not melting." But we were just getting along at that time. That's before I was in the fire department.

It was pretty close to the Irvington line and most of Irvington was that way too. Nice, nice people, although over on Nineteenth Avenue they were no longer Irish and German, but they were Polish and Ukrainian, a lot of different mixtures of people. But Newark was good to me, Newark was always good to me. I think back, we had a lot of good things. My wife was in the First Ward over on Garside Street. She always brags she could come home at twelve o'clock at night. Take the bus and get off at Mount Prospect Avenue, come down Third Avenue, walk on Garside Street and have no fear of anybody bothering her. Nobody would molest her or anything else.

Carragher: (appointed 1960) Oh, it was beautiful. It was just starting to slide a little bit then, in the '60es. I lived in North Newark on Summer Avenue and Summer Avenue was a beautiful street. We knew everybody. Everybody around the neighborhood were all friends. Our family was active in church over at Saint Michael's Church in Newark. We had theaters. We had the burlesque shows, bars. Anything you wanted to do you could do in Newark at the time. It was probably in the early '60s when it started really changing. I moved to Newark in 1946 and from '46 until the time I came on the job, I really enjoyed the city of Newark. It was really good.

Harris: (appointed 1961) Well, I moved to Newark when I was eight years old. I came from East Rutherford, New Jersey. I came to Newark after my father died. My mom couldn't keep the house and we moved to Newark. Newark when I was growing up, you went to the same schools. The schools weren't segregated. I believe schools were better then because you went to school and there were "x" black in the class and the teachers taught. They were ninety percent white teachers in the schools. You as a student learned as well as the white students did because they taught you. Over the years, you can see how it's changed. I would say the school system now is about seventy percent minority teachers and they're out of the schools before the kids are out. The system and the kids' grades are down. But when I was going to school it wasn't like that.

If I came home with a bad grade, forget about it. I got my butt whipped and you better sit down. You better study. You're on punishment. You don't do this. You had to do your lessons. There were no ifs, ands, or buts. You did it. You couldn't stay home from school because at that time they had truant officers. Today they would send letters home. You get home. You intercept them before your mom sees them. But the truant officer came to the door and knocked on the door and told your mother, "He ain't been to school." That's how it was.

Back then you had movie theaters. We had the Regent down on Bloomfield Avenue at Bloomfield and Broad. There was the Embassy at the top of Bloomfield Avenue. There was the Elwood movie up in North Newark on Elwood Avenue and Broad. And then you had the five movies downtown. But growing up in the city of Newark, you as a minority or black sat in certain sections of the movies in the city of Newark. Then slowly it changed. Also growing up in the city of Newark, we used to walk from North Newark where the seventy-seven steps are up to Summer Avenue and to Mount Prospect Avenue. We used to go up there. Then nine times out of ten, we'd have to fight from there to Branch Brook Park. We were fighting with the Italian kids because that was their neighborhood. Then we'd come back. You may have to fight just to come back. But that's what we did growing up if we wanted to go to Branch Brook Park.

Basically, in North Newark all your blacks lived below Summer Avenue, Delavan, Summer, Wilburton and down Oraton Street. Then down in the old First Ward you had about three streets where blacks lived. Like Julius Banks, he lived on Webster Street right next to Anthony "Tony" Imperiele when they were growing up. Before I even came on the job, Emile Nardone was my mailman. That's how I knew Emile before coming into the job. And his father owned a store on Broadway, a candy store. He sold sodas and candy and stuff like that. We used to go in there because the church we went to, Clinton Memorial, was right across the street from Tony's father's store. That's how I knew Tony and Emile, from there. That's how Newark was years ago.

Newark was divided up at that time. We had what we called the "hill." Now the hill was Prince, Spruce, Belmont, Eighteenth, Waverly, all the way down to Avon Avenue that whole area. It wasn't in two blocks on the other side of Clinton Avenue going south. And then you had a lot of blacks who lived off Bergen Street going up to just above Six Engine, Hunterdon Street around in there. Now right on the other side of where Camden Street is, where the school is today, Fourteenth, Thirteenth, and Seventeenth that was strictly another Italian neighborhood all in that area. In North Newark we lived from Clay Street all below Broadway going back to Elwood Avenue.

Everybody lived below Broad Street. Coming back, cross town you had what we called the "valley," Pennsylvania Avenue, Sherman Avenue. There was about a ten-block area where blacks lived down there. No blacks lived in the Burg. Forget about it. You didn't live up there. We used to call it "mortgage hill" when I came on the job because all your civil servants, Police and Fire, lived in Vailsburg. We couldn't go up there and get the mortgage. Forest Hills, North Newark, you didn't live there. The Weequachic section, forget about it. It was interesting.

Haran: (appointed 1961) I grew up in the Roseville section on Seventh Avenue. It runs parallel with Orange Street, which was a main street at that particular time. I can remember the tracks in the street going back then. They used to have trolley cars. The downtown area had all the electrical wires strung across Broad Street. That's the way it was back then. I had two brothers and two sisters. We all attended the same school, which was Saint Rose of Lima School on Orange Street and Humbolt Street.

That part of life circled around Saint Rose of Lima's. We were all in the choir. We were all altar boys. We all attended mass there. My two sisters and both my brothers were married in Saint Rose of Lima's. I was married in the Scared Heart Cathedral down on Clifton Avenue and Sixth Avenue because my wife was from that area down there. My whole life revolved around the school at that particular time. My sisters graduated. They went on to other schools and I came to the down neck area. I went to Saint James High School. Then out of high school, I went to the phone company and then from the phone company I came to the fire department. So, I grew up in the Roseville section, which was a nice section at the time.

The makeup of Newark back then was predominantly white, but there were pockets of African-Americans in the area. They were over in the next block from me. There was no trouble back then and none to be expected. Really, everybody got along. The area that I grew up in was predominantly Italian and Irish, probably mostly Irish. There wasn't much to do. We didn't have much. Everybody was in the same boat. We all thought this was the way life was, but everybody was just hard working families there. Our weekends when I was a kid were spent down at Branch Brook Park. That's where we used to go all the time.

Up until my mid-teens, until I started driving at seventeen, most of my time was spent in that particular area. You didn't go too far out of your area. You had no means of getting out unless you walked. But mostly my friends and everything we needed to do or wanted to do was in that area. There were movie theaters. I think today there are only two movie theaters in the city of Newark, but back then I think there were as many as fifty. On Saturdays everybody went to the movie. Sundays we went to church. Friday night was CYO when I was a teenager. That was basically it. We didn't move too far out. I didn't know too much of the city. I used to take a bus to high school, so I traveled from the Roseville section, which was considered the North Ward then, down to Saint James High School, which was in the Ironbound section. Today the Roseville section isn't considered the North Ward anymore. It's in the Central Ward section now. They broke it up years ago.

You could get anything you wanted in the city of Newark back then. There was everything. There was manufacturing. We had a seaport second to none. We had a thriving airport. Today it's an international airport. It's probably one of the four top airports in the country today. Anything you wanted to buy, you could get in the city of Newark. With the manufacturing, you didn't have to go any place else. In the downtown area, we had big department stores. We had Bamberger's, which is Macy's now, but it used to be known as Bamberger's. We had Ohrbach's. We had S.Klien on the square. We had Hahne's. They were located in the center of the city and could be reached from any outskirts of the city in fifteen, twenty minutes on a bus. You didn't have to go anyplace else. There were no malls back then. Anything you wanted, you could get in the city of Newark. And busy, busy back then. I think when I came on and growing up in the city of Newark, I don't think the population ever hit five hundred thousand. But it came close. Today it's only somewhere around two hundred and fifty thousand, but back then it was like five hundred thousand. Not only that, but with all the stores we had there and all the manufacturing in the Ironbound section and other parts of the city, I think the city used to swell to a million and a half people during the day. We had a lot of people in the city of Newark. And the fire department had to protect all those people. It was quite a responsibility.

Cahill: (appointed 1963) I spent my whole life in Newark. We lived in the Roseville section and then moved up to the Burg. I really didn't appreciate the differences. In the end you see the potential changes coming. You could see everything little by little, creeping. But basically as a kid it was a great city.

Highsmith: (appointed 1963) At that time the city was nice. I liked it. Everybody was friendly. There were no big problems around. We had quite a few fires because we had quite a few frame houses, but the city was in good condition. The joke was everybody was happy. Not a lot of crime, no problem with the kids in school. Nothing like it is today.

Butler: (appointed 1963) I had been born and raised in the city and I thought the city was still a relatively nice place to live. Probably be a good place to work and you look forward to a career in firefighting. At the time I came on the job, it was still predominantly white. I remember when I first went on Central Avenue there was one black family living on Ninth Street between Central Avenue and Ninth Avenue. Nice gentleman with his family, knew all the firemen. I would say within two to three weeks of being there I was introduced to him. Saw his kids grow up. Very nice, he was a hard working man. His wife was working. Nice kids, they all went on to be professionals, doctor, lawyer, and a psychologist. His daughter turned out to be a psychologist.

Cody: (appointed 1964) I'm from Newark. I grew up in the First Ward on High Street, High Street and Seventh Avenue. We lived there and then we moved up to Sussex Avenue and then we moved over to Fourth Street right near Orange Street. That's where we lived when I came on the job. I went to Saint Michael's over here. I graduated from Saint Michael's. It was predominantly Italian. I was the token Irish kid that in the neighborhood. I remember getting beat up a couple of times just walking up Eighth Avenue.

That area was really great. It had all the feasts and it had just so many people. They were just always out of their homes. They knock it all down for the projects. It all centered around Saint Lucy's.

We used to walk downtown all the time. This is when I was a kid. It was still nice. When I came on the fire department I moved to Vailsburg. I got married. We had a home up in Vailsburg and we used to go downtown all the time. The city was nice. There was a lot of shopping. All the department stores were down there.

Garrity: (appointed 1964) The city was a great place when I came on. There were places to go, things to do all day, all night long, a great place. I enjoyed the city a lot. Always some place, something to do.

Knight: (appointed 1964) The makeup of the city at that time was all Jewish in Weequahic. There weren't that many blacks. The blacks hadn't moved in over there yet. They were mostly down in the heart of the Central Ward. Up in the West Ward there was an ethnic mix of Italians, Irish, Polish, Germans, and Ukrainians. Where I lived was a mixture, a lot of Irish. We had different things in the city and you had more time to enjoy yourself

Wargo: (appointed 1964) The city at the time, wasn't a lot different than it was before I went into the service. Of course, the style had changed, but everything else was still here. The movie theaters were all here; the big stores Kresge's, Hayne's, Bamberger's, and American Shops. All those stores that I knew as a young person, they were still here. The city was still flourishing and everything seemed safe. It was just a good place to live.

I wasn't born in Newark, but I spent most of my life in Newark in the Ironbound. It was made up of the Dutch neck and the Irish neck. It was sort of chopped up into ethnic areas, but in my area over near St. Casper's there were a lot of Polish people, with a lot of Italian mixed in, and some Irish. There weren't many blacks. The black families who lived down neck had been there for a long, long time. So they were really natives of the area. They had lived there for generations. It was a good makeup. It was a good mix. I went to Catholic grammar school, which at the time was all white because of the neighborhood. But right across the street from that was East Side and that was mixed. It was Spanish, Portuguese, Italian, German and

Slovens, Sumerians, Polish, and some black and some Jewish. It was a mix. It was a melting pot. It was down neck.

McGovern: (appointed 1968) Newark was neighborhoods. Down neck was Irish, German, and Polish at the time. Very rarely did down neck people go up above the wall. You went uptown to shop, go to a movie once and a while, but other than that you stayed in your neighborhood. That's the way it was. Not many people had cars. The guy who had the car, he was your only escape. You used buses. But it was all a neighborhood type of thing. North Newark was Italian. Down neck was mixed. Vailsburg was mixed. I'd say the city was seventy-five percent white, twenty-five percent minority at the time.

D. Prachar: (appointed 1968) I grew up in a mixed neighborhood on Alpine Street. The house next door was always black. The house across the street was always black. It wasn't until certain types of black people moved into the neighborhood that a neighborhood changed. Prime example is Willie Curry in Nineteen Engine. His family moved into Sherman Avenue and Alpine Street. They weren't accepted by the people in the neighborhood because it was a big family as far as the amount of kids. Willie even says, when he moved in on Alpine Street, if you weren't liked by the Prachars, you got beat up, because my brother used to beat him up all the time. And then finally it became an accepted thing. The Currys were there. There was nothing you were going to do to move them out. So, then your neighborhood started changing. Not because of the Currys, but because it was cheap to live in that area.

Cosby: (appointed 1969) I wasn't born in Newark. I was born in Florida, the State of Florida. I moved to Newark in 1958. When I first came to Newark I really didn't like it because where I lived before was basically one-family homes. I could never get used to living in a house with someone else, like a multiple dwelling, someone living on the top of you and the bottom. It took me a long time to get used to that. At that time I would say Newark was at least seventy percent white and thirty percent minority. I didn't realize that there was a lot of discrimination in the city of Newark. Coming from out of the south you always heard that the north was like paradise compared to the south as far as race relations.

One thing that really stood out in my mind was the newspaper advertisements. I'll never forget it. I remember when we had the Newark Evening News. There were people who would advertise apartments for rent. Whenever they want a white person for the apartment, they would list the apartment as say a three-bedroom apartment, kitchen. Then they would put in there, "white stove, white refrigerator." What that really meant was that they wanted a white person for that apartment. That's the way they would get around the law. They couldn't put white person, white only. So they would put that in the ad. That was the negative side. There were some positive sides. I think that kind of situation more or less made me work harder. I'm not the type who would try to buck anything like that. I mean it made it difficult for you, but what it did for me is inspire me to purchase a house. I purchased my first house when I was twenty-four years old. That was my way of solving the housing situation. I just went out and bought a house.

McDonnell: (appointed 1970) I grew up in Newark. I was born in 1943 and lived in the city my entire life, up until then. I lived in a lot of different places because we moved quite a bit before I was about ten. I lived on Eleventh Street by South Orange Avenue, the Central Ward and Fourteenth and South Orange Avenue until I was six. Then I lived downtown. I lived over on Clinton Avenue, back downtown, up on Ninth Avenue, back downtown, and then when I was ten years old we moved to the projects in North Newark. I lived there for eleven years. At the time I came on the job I lived in North Newark. I was living on Clifton Avenue.

It was a city that was in decline. It started I guess to decline in the '50s. Probably hit its peak in the '40s, early '50s and things started to change. The population started to change, the city started to go downhill. We had a big welfare population. People were moving up from down south. The city started to go into decline in the late '50s, continued to the '60s, and with the riots accelerated. The population change was dramatic after the riots. Things changed dramatically. People left the city in droves. Right after that there was a big, big exodus from the city. There was an exodus of businesses. I think the biggest population change had already taken place by the time I came on the job.

North Newark was a white area, Vailsburg was a white area, but the South and Central Wards were pretty much black. I don't think there were too many white people left over in the Weequahic section. The major population change had taken place. The racial make-up was probably sixty-forty. Sixty percent black, forty percent whites and a little Hispanic population maybe filled in five percent of that. It was probably at that point that the city was just on the brink of almost hitting bottom. It probably hit bottom in the next ten to fifteen years. The businesses were still all of downtown. They weren't empty, but Springfield Avenue, which was a major business street, was probably half empty. The whole Central Ward was on its skids, abandoned buildings galore. The city was definitely in a state of decline.

Melodick: (appointed 1970) I am a Newark boy. I grew up here. In 1955 I lived on Camden Street and South Orange Avenue. I was six years old. Do I love the City? Yes, I love it. I think it was the best place to live if you could live here, but things have changed. I know crime wasn't like the way it was later on. I remember walking with my mother and father up and down Springfield Avenue. Went to Camden Street School, went to Alexander Street then I went to Vailsburg, had no problems ever. Things have changed. Obviously now you have to live other places besides Newark. But if I had my choice, I'd come back here any time to live. It was fun. It was fun living here, something about city life. The people, they're closer. They share. Everybody knows one another. It seems like when you move out to the suburbs, everybody's a distance apart. Everybody keeps to themselves. But to me city life is the best. Plus you learn. You become street smart and you learn many things about life that most of these kids in the suburbs have no idea. They might be book smart, but not about life.

Pianka: (appointed 1970) I was raised in Newark down neck. I spent most of my youth, below the wall, below Penn Station. Mostly white, I knew the black people were up in the Central Ward, but it was two different worlds. Never got intimate with black people until I came here to the fire department.

Rotonda: (appointed 1970) Fantastic. I grew up in Newark; went to Central High School in Newark. Used to go roller-skating over in Dreamland. Switch buses downtown Newark and stop for ice cream at

Brandford Place. I think it was Seams or something at the time. Ice cream, a whole bunch of people from school and everywhere else, we'd all meet up in Dreamland. But the city of Newark, was fantastic. Couldn't beat it.

The whole city was ethnic. You had the Irish section. You had the Jewish section. You had the Italian section. You had the Polish section. You never knew how sheltered a life you lived until you grew up and moved out of the city and found out everybody wasn't Italian. Ivy Hill was more or less the Irish section. North Newark was the Italian section. Weequahic was the Jewish section and down neck was predominantly Polish. It was all mixed in between, but the predominance of the ethnic backgrounds made it good. I covered the whole city of Newark in the sausage business and then with Coca-Cola before I came on this job. So I'm pretty well versed in the city of Newark.

T. Grehl: (appointed 1971) I grew up in the Vailsburg section of Newark. Part of my house was in Irvington, my garage was actually in Irvington. My house was in Newark, so I had kind of like the best of everything. I went to grammar school at Saint Leo's in Irvington. Then I played all my sports and spent a lot of my time in Vailsburg Park with the guys from Newark. So, I had a combination of both types of friends, from Catholic school and the public school. Vailsburg Park was where we spent all our time.

Where I grew up was a combination. It was a mixture of everybody, all different nationalities, all different religions, some old people, some young people coming in, Irish, Italian. The Vailsburg section was predominantly white. From basically the Parkway west, the West Ward, was predominantly white. South Orange Avenue had a little more of an Italian area. North Newark was the Italian area. Over by Weequahic High School was the Jewish area. Down neck at the time was more Polish and then Portuguese began coming in. I used to go to the doctor down there.

We shopped in Newark on Springfield Avenue. The toy store was on Springfield Avenue right down the street from Six Engine. The shoe store was there. The clothing stores, David Burr's, a couple of other ones were up in Irvington Center. The sporting goods store was Duviga's across the street from Bamberger's and it was Hayne's and Kresge's and the five and ten and a lot of little stores. But there were no malls. We got on the fifty-four Devine and took it right down to downtown Newark. That's where we spent our Saturdays shopping for our parents for Christmas and for their birthdays.

We did everything in Newark, everything. Movies were in Newark, a little bit of Irvington Center. There was the Castle in Irvington and then there was the Sanford on South Orange Avenue. That was the movie theater I went to with the Newark people. When I went with the Irvington people it was the Castle. But everything was right there. The furniture stores were on South Orange Avenue in Vailsburg. Everything was there. Anything you wanted.

Then when the riots came, obviously that changed quite a bit. A lot of those little mom and pop stores along Springfield Avenue were no longer there. They left because of the change in the city or because of vandalism and they couldn't rebuild or whatever. Downtown Newark started changing when the malls came. When Willowbrook Mall was built, that really hurt downtown Newark, more so than the riots. Because everybody still went to Bamberger's, still went to Hayne's, but when the malls came and they put the Bamberger's up in Willowbrook Mall that's where you went. So it took away the heart of downtown.

When I first came on the job it was only four years after the riots. So the memory of the riots was still very, very visible. Everybody could see it.

The Ironbound section below that wall, below McCarter Highway was a stand-offish point. The buildings were burnt out in the Central Ward. There was still a tremendous amount of fires. So the after-glow of the riots was still around. A lot of people were very, very prejudice and had hard feelings. The hard feelings were there. It was obvious that the city was in turmoil. It wasn't ready to bounce back yet in '70, '71, '72.

Ryan: (appointed 1973) I loved the city when I was growing up. It was great fun. I used to walk back and forth to school on South Orange Avenue. As a kid of seven or eight we thought nothing of telling our parents that we were going to go downtown, get a movie, and we would ride on the Thirty-one Dover Street down and go to the movie and come home. Played a lot in Vailsburg Park except when the Army camp was there during the Korean War. Hardly anybody remembers that. There was an entire Army camp in Vailsburg Park during the Korean War and there were quite a number of soldiers that were there.

Vailsburg was a great place to grow up. I enjoyed it thoroughly. It was loaded with cops and firemen. We lived in the projects on North Munn Avenue for seven years of my existence and then we moved up to eighty-five Monticello where we remained the rest of the time, right on the corner of Marian and Monticello. My grandfather lived next door. Denny Carry, Director of Public Safety lived immediately behind us.

I still had a lot of friends down in the projects and we used to go down and play. It was more open spaces in Vailsburg Park and it was easier to get down there than it was to go up to Ivy Hill Park. We thought nothing of walking around. There was a great hobby store on the corner of Alexander and South Orange. Picked up models, used to build models there. My dad used to work part time in Sussex Brake on the corner of Munn and South

Orange. So, we were constantly back and forth. That was another reason I was going down to that area to play in the park. The park was great. It was wide open and a nice park, except when the Army was there. They had big search light trucks and everything.

Newark's always been a city of immigrants, which a lot of people find that hard to believe. Whether one group or the other predominates for a given period of time, it always changes. It's a regular cycle in the city. It's just by the nature of the industry that's in the town, the jobs that are available. Certain parts of the city were Italian or German or Polish or Black or just about anything. There were very diverse communities in the city. It wasn't predominated by any one group at all. And it was a very stable and very nice place to grow up. I see it coming back to that now. I really do. I see a large influx of Hispanics and Europeans from places you never really hear about. Newark, New Jersey is the third largest receiving place in the country for immigrants from Poland. Polish as a second language is still taught in the Ann Street and Wilson Avenue schools.

Langenbach: (appointed 1973) The city was the pits when I came on the job. Belmont Avenue was like a war zone. It still was all the vacant buildings. There were still some things left. I think there was one, maybe two bakeries behind the firehouse. I know the pillow factory was back there. There were a couple of white bakeries back there, German, whatever they were. But everything around us was burnt out pretty much.

Connell: (appointed 1974) Basically, down neck is what it is now. It was mostly Portuguese. The center part of the town was basically black. Around Bloomfield Avenue, the Hispanic population was moving in and Vailsburg was still basically white with the blacks starting to infringe on it.

Perdon: (appointed 1974) The city was all I knew. I didn't know anything else. We were the type of people, we didn't have money. So, even our vacations were like they weren't there. Newark was my whole life. I went to Essex Catholic. I went to a Catholic grammar school. Then I went to Essex Catholic High. Everything was all Newark related. I thought it was really fine. Like I said, I knew nothing else. I didn't even know what Vailsburg was like. That was on the other side of that wall. My life was on that side of the wall. Until I came on the fire department, well I went into the service in between, but then the fire department. That was it. We had the riots, '67, other than that, normal growing up type of experiences.

Bisogna: (appointed 1974) I grew up in Vailsburg. I got married. I lived there for a couple of years after I came on the job. I had a lot of friends in Vailsburg. Tree lined streets, a lot of kids hanging out. At the playground where I hung out there were thirty, forty, fifty guys. Sometimes three o'clock in the morning, you'd go by there, there'd be forty people standing there. We always used to kid around, you punched in, punched out. We'd come and hang out and punched a clock, put your hours in for the day. It was a good place to grow up.

We had a reunion not too long ago at Cryan's up in South Orange. I'll bet you there were three hundred people. A lot of them were from my year or right around my year. Just seeing people twenty-five years later, it would have been nice if the neighborhood could have been sustained; everybody buying homes in the area because it was like Cheers. You went to Cryan's and all your friends were sitting at the table. If you went to the next bar, you knew a group of guys there. It was fun to grow up like that, have a place to hang out. Not making bars as being the place to be, but there was more of a social aspect to it. Knowing a lot of people is always fun. Vailsburg was nice. The homes were well kept. It was a working class neighborhood, a lot of cops and firemen, Irish, Italian.

Like I said I lived in Newark when I came on the job and I thought it was a good place to live, It was after the riots, so there was a lot of destruction in the Central Ward. Driving through it to go to high school, you saw a lot of changes. It was pretty disgusting, but I didn't have to get off the bus. The bus took me to Essex Catholic, which was on the other side of town. It was still pretty decent over there too at the time.

Working on Prince Street and looking around, you saw there were a lot of abandoned buildings at the time. It's much improved in the last twenty-five, twenty-seven years, a lot of changes. For a while it was the Great Plains there, by Five Truck you could just look for miles. Turn your head you could see nothing but high rises. A lot of stuff was knocked down. There was block after block vacant, just dirt. But now there are townhouses. It's amazing. The last time I went down Irvine Turner it's a whole different area. It's really something.

Ricca: (appointed 1974) North Newark where I grew up on Montclair Avenue right down from Summer was probably the greatest place in the world to live. I'm sure all of us who came from certain sections believe that. But there was Elliot Street School a block away for the playground. Of course, we played stick ball in the street even though the playground was around the corner. Branch Brook Park was two to three blocks away. There was an old church, called the old Italian Church for no other reason but to call it the old Italian Church. That was on Summer Avenue and there were two lots. We played in the church lot. We played there from morning until night. Eventually they knocked the church down and built the thing known now as the Immaculate Conception Church on Woodside and Montclair.

But you couldn't get in trouble because from my house to the lot I had to pass three or four relatives houses, two neighbors who were close friends and a couple of neighbors that weren't close friends, but if you did something wrong you either got reprimanded by the neighbor or got whacked by him, because that's how they were back then. The families were very close. It was nothing for your aunt to wind up and whack you if you were doing wrong. A few times it happened to me. That changed. That's I think the main reason why the cities and even the suburbs aren't what they used to be.

We used to go to the bakery on Summer Avenue with a nickel and buy a loaf of Italian bread. Bring it to the butcher across the street, for a quarter he'd fill it with spiced ham and cheese, and for thirty cents you had two or three guys eating off a sandwich. A huge, big old sandwich and then if you bought mustard, the butcher would keep it in his refrigerator for you, put it on your sandwich when you went in the next time. The butcher lived down the block too.

At this time, North Newark was the Italian section with Broadway black and Hispanic. The Archbishop Walsh projects everybody swore was the ruination of North Newark because we found at a later date that a high rise is a bad type situation to put people into. You know that from the Hayes Homes, the Stella Wrights, and all the projects that are gone right now.

From Broadway up to I guess Mount Prospect Avenue or Clifton Avenue was considered North Newark. Then above Clifton was considered Forest Hill. That's where you go trick or treating on Halloween because you got true nickel candy bars. If you went out with a girl from Forest Hill you were considered doing good. The rivalry always came between Elliot Street School which is on Summer Avenue and Ridge Street School which is on Ridge Street. I had that go round and round with Bobby Testa over that. That he was one of the rich kids from Ridge Street and we were the poor kids down in the valley. But predominantly, I'd say the neighborhood I grew up in was ninety percent Italian at the time, from store owners to street sweepers.

People think I'm crazy, but I remember when the rag man came by and had a horse. I'm forty-seven, but the rag man came by with his horse to pick up rags. The umbrella man would come ringing the bell as he walked the street, sharpening your knives and fix your umbrella. The fish man, the soda man, there was a Jewish fellow who came by, March is his last name. I can't think of his first name, but he actually opened the back of his truck and put steps up and he would walk the women in and out of his truck and sold clothing right from the back of his truck. The Fuller brush man, you couldn't wait for one of these salesmen to come to the house because they would give you a whistle or something crazy, trying to sell your mother a vacuum cleaner or whatever the wares were. I guess as I got into my teens the neighborhood started to change with a little mix of mostly Hispanic.

The Blue Max was the big gang around then. If they came walking into your neighborhood, they had their colors on, it was almost like the Westside Story going back. Where, they would only walk in pairs in our neighborhood. We were only supposed to walk in pairs in their neighborhood, the whole turf thing. When I look back at it, the stupidity of it, but it was just the way things were. Every corner had its own gang. I guess my generation grew out of wearing the colors, the vest with the insignia on the back, but my brothers went through that. Angelo, God rest his soul, with his group used to wear motorcycle jackets and motorcycle hats and not one of them had a motorcycle. But that was the way they dressed. I guess the Marlon Brando look. I don't even know the name of the movie he was in, but Marlon Brando had the cap with the motorcycle jacket.

In a minute I'd go back to living there again if I could have it the way it was. I guess we all would. I bring my kids through. My daughter just graduated college. When she was two we moved from Newark, but when you ask her where she's from, she's from Newark. She's proud of it even though she only lived there two years, so she doesn't remember. She thinks she does. But Newark just carries a stigma with it for some people. When you live here and you grew up here, there's a pride that you came from Newark.

Back then it was a one car family. You had to take a bus, so the only time I ventured out of the area was on bike; we used to take bicycle runs. Everybody would have a bike, jump on it. I'm ashamed to say I was so used to just being in my neighborhood, I got lost on Mill Street in Belleville. We had a half dozen of us on bikes. We were at Mill Street where it hits Belleville Avenue and there was a pizzeria on the corner. We stood there almost in tears wondering how we were going to get home because nobody remembered the route we took. But we would go down near Seventh Avenue. That was a shopping center back then. It was closer than downtown and the bus was a nickel. We used to call it the cheap Charlie bus. It was the Eighteen. It was five cents. It was independent transit and every Friday my mother would take me and my sister down. You'd go to McCrory's because you couldn't eat meat on Friday if you were Catholic. You'd have a slice of pizza or they had a fish fry and you would go shopping there. But usually on a close run you'd go down by Seventh Avenue and Bloomfield Place where Petskin's is and they had everything you wanted there. You didn't have to go downtown. But a Friday would be the trek to downtown for the pizza and fish fry via bus. My mother sewed. She's a very good sewer and there was a fabric shop there down near Seventh Avenue. During the week if she needed anything, she'd send me out. Bloomfield Avenue was my limit. I couldn't cross Bloomfield Avenue until I was about fifteen.

Restrictions were put on you back then. The big thing was when you got your license. Being a good Italian, you'd put your parking lights on. You'd hang your hand out the window and give the gangster lean. You would start at the Dairy Queen and if you drove at thirty-five miles an hour you'd beat every light up to Bloomfield where you made a turn. You went to Willie's State Diner, had cake, you came back down and made the loop again. The same people that were hanging on each corner on Bloomfield Avenue when you went up were there when you came down. It was just a series of beeping the horn and waving and seeing who knew the most people. You couldn't wait. It was almost inbreeded in every kid that I grew up with. As soon as you got your license, pop, your parking lights went on and you just headed for the Avenue.

I got my license in 1970. I wasn't even allowed to be in a friend's car until I was sixteen. My friend Billy Shadle, I'll never forget the kid, phenomenal baseball player. He got a '63 Riviera and that's all we ever did was drive up and down Bloomfield Avenue. And at the end of the night, I'd give him a dollar for gas. He'd put a dollar in and we'd get a half a tank of gas. Because they had the price wars, every gas station was thirty cents, twenty-nine cents, a quarter.

But as a young kid, leaving the area, you didn't have to. You went to school in your neighborhood so all your friends were in the neighborhood. Like now my kids had friends all over the map, all over the town of Bloomfield which is a pretty decent size town. But back then you kind of stayed in your group. It was like the Little Rascals almost. You had a nick name for everybody. People didn't have a whole lot of money then, so it wasn't like now. Most of the time, when lunch was called you headed home. Everybody went to their own houses, ate and fifteen minutes later everybody was back.

The part of Branch Brook Park known as the extensions or the four diamonds as we called it, the four baseball fields, that's where you'd be most of the summer. You'd be in the early morning up there playing ball. There was no Little League. Nothing organized. You'd make teams up. Put a screw in a bat that broke, wooden bat then, not aluminum. You'd tape the hardball together and you played. Then you'd come down after you ate supper. You'd go local, to the church lot, and you'd hang out there for the rest of the night. People sat on their porches so coming in at eleven, twelve at night was no big deal because as long as your parents were on the porch you were allowed to be out. That's how I was brought up.

It started changing in the early '70s. During the Newark riots I was in summer school at Essex Catholic. That was in 1967. And there was a sniper in the building. The Brother came on the loud speaker and told everyone to leave via the Summer Avenue exit and not to take any buses down on Broadway. He never told anybody that there was a sniper up in the school. Could it have been a story made up by some of the kids? Possibly, but I left by Summer Avenue and ran up to Mount Prospect Avenue to get the Twenty-seven. I noticed right after the riots my friends started thinning out. The old saying was, "Where are all those good Italians from Newark? Belleville and Bloomfield." That's where people took off to and that's how the neighborhood broke up.

I ended up with a lot of Hispanic friends. Good people who moved to the area where I lived in North Newark to get away from being in the projects and everything. They were working people. Their parents worked just as hard mine did, raised their kids the same. One kid, his name was Archio, I'll never forget, his mother would come out and hit him in the head, if she heard somebody curse in Spanish. Because he was the only Spanish kid at the time, if she heard Spanish cursing, she knew it was him. She'd come out and she'd chase him around.

But right after the riots I noticed it, realized it. The older people were dieing, selling their houses, and their sons and daughters were moving. Or people would flat out move, take loses on their houses at the time because I think real estate was bad. I guess that's from '70 to '75, I think the neighborhood changed drastically. The bodegas came in. The old Italian butcher died and his shop was sold off to Hispanic.

Gesualdo: (appointed 1978) Well, everything was regional back then. In those days you had your Italian section, your Irish section, your black section. I grew up in the Italian section, which was North Newark where the old First Ward was as they called it. I remember it being pleasant. I had a good time. Everybody around there was family basically. People next door, across the street, down the block, never any problems. If you had a situation that you needed help, you just knocked at anybody's door. I remember people on the streets at night, sitting on porches, having little groups, not gangs, but little groups of guys that hung together. Occasional problems, you know, sneaking the smokes, the drinking, things like that, but pretty much it was a normal childhood, a lot of athletics, playing stickball in the street and porch ball, football in the corner lot. So, pretty much a normal neighborhood from what I knew until I started branching out and getting my license and finding out what the other sections of Newark were like. I mean, if you go to Vailsburg, it was a trek or to go down neck was a kind of experience because it was a totally different environment than you were used to. But I don't remember too many places going back in the late '50s, early '60s where there were many problems. It was a great upbringing. You had all your cousins and friends around you all the time, family. So it was a good place to grow up. Lot of good restaurants.

My area was pretty much ninety-five percent Caucasian whatever, Mediterranean. I know when we used to go across Orange Street, that was kind of like the dividing line. That's where the black area started around Baxter Terrace and all that. When they took Eighth Avenue out to build the 280 highway that was kind of like the dividing line. You knew if you went across the highway that there was a pretty good chance you were going to get into some kind of fight or something because you just didn't go there and they didn't come across Eighth Avenue, the old Eighth Avenue. So, at the time I would say probably it was as far as minorities go, however you want to classify them, I'd say maybe at that time it was sixty forty maybe. What they considered to be white or Caucasian or Italian or whatever compared to black and Hispanic. I believe now it's probably up closer to eighty percent minority maybe twenty percent Caucasian.

The West Ward used to be all Irish. We used to go up there for dances occasionally by the old Sacred Heart Church. That was mostly Irish white up there. Central Ward was mostly where you're minorities were and the lower end of the North section down around McCarter Highway. So, I would say from the time I grew up in, it was maybe sixty forty when I was going into the service. When I came out it started growing closer to seventy. Now I'd say it's probably about eighty to twenty maybe minority to white.

Chapter Two: Why a Fireman?

Fredette: Well, for one thing the excitement; the security; and a lot of friends I met in the tavern were firemen and they seemed to like the job so I said that is the job for me. When we got appointed it was during the war. If not for the war, lots of guys and lots of chiefs would have never been on. They talked about only appointing twenty-five policemen and twenty-five firemen at the time. Things were tough with the depression and the older men were looking for a raise in pay. They didn't want any new guys coming on and taking their raise in pay. That was when we got on.

Vetrini: I married into a fire department family. My father-in-law was a fire captain and his son was a firefighter. The brother in law, who had married one of my wife's sisters, he was a firefighter. Then I became a temporary in 1946. I was wounded in service; came out while the war was still on. When the war ended I went on as a temporary, January the first 1946. And then became a regular off the second list for inductees from Civil Service. That was in July 1, 1948.

A State law at that time said if anybody is a temporary employee and a veteran wants to apply for that job, the temporary employee had to relinquish the job to the veteran. During the war they were inducting men from the Police and Fire Departments. This prevailed throughout the country. They had to put a stop to it because they were depleting the departments of able-bodied men. A lot of the fellows who were on the job were frozen to the job. After taking so many men they had to hire people, so they hired temporary fire fighters. Then when fellows like myself came home, we were able to take the temporary fire fighter positions. There were ten of us. One of the fellows on the list, Artie Knipsel, was the first firefighter who was put on to the 1944 Act as a regular employee. He took the job with the medal that he got, the Navy Cross.

I took the job for security and I took it as a temporary just because my father-in-law said, "Would you like to be a firefighter?" So I said "I'll give it a try." Of course, I was working as a disabled veteran. I could pick any job I wanted. I was working for the Internal Revenue at the time. I gave it a try. As a temporary, I liked it, so then I took the written for Civil Service. Being a disabled veteran, I was up in the top five or six. That is basically it. I saw that the family was in it and they seemed to like it and it had security. No two ways about it.

Redden: I wanted a steady job. Before I went in the service I worked the shipyards in Kearny. When I got out of the service in '46, I went back to the shipyards, but of course there was not much need for cruisers and destroyers at that time so I got laid off. I held a couple of jobs. I worked in Kresge's as a maintenance man for a couple of months. The exam came up. I took it and I was appointed off of that list.

Kinnear: I don't remember any specific reason why I became a fireman. I was in the service. When I got back in January 1946, I went to college. I was going on an accelerated program because I had lost three years in the service. I couldn't get back into studying really. I wanted to makeup for those three years by having a little fun, I guess. I didn't realize that college required so much. When the fire department test came up, my father being a Battalion Chief said, "Why don't you take the test?" I took it without any real feeling that I wanted the job. I finished within the top fifty. When the job was offered, I figured I'd give it a shot. I gave it a try and I liked it, so that's basically how I became a fireman.

Masters: Well, I took quite a few exams. I took the police, fire, state troopers. After the war there were a lot of vacancies in all fields. I even took prison guard. But I figured I didn't commit a crime, why stay in prison for ten, twenty years. So, I picked the fire department and I'm glad I did.

F. Grehl: That's a tough question because when I got out of the service, I had a civil service job working for the Internal Revenue Service. My father was a fireman. They were working eighty-four hours a week at the time and he tried to persuade me not to take the fire department because of the great hours and reduced pay that I would have started with. I think it intrigued me because I was used to it my whole life. Right from school I was drafted into the Army and then right out of the Army I took that civil service test. But I still liked outdoor life rather than working behind a desk which I did for a year and a half in the Internal Revenue Service.

The excitement was part of it. I was in the Army infantry during the war. So there was always a lot of excitement, always a lot of outdoor, and it became very tranquil when I went and took a desk job. Also, when I got out of the service it was too late to start the fall semester in college. I started going nights at Seton Hall to further my education. I was studying accounting at the time. Of course, the courses helped me with the Internal Revenue Service and what I was doing. But after a year and a half of that and after the fire department came up I decided I didn't want to stay indoors and work.

Even when I was working for the IRS I did a lot of work outdoors. There was an outfit called War Assets Administration that sold surplus materials. I did a lot of the auditing in the various surplus depots through out the east. That's how I got started in that. Then when they sold all the surplus materials we dissolved the whole unit. That's when they transferred me to the Internal Revenue Service in New York City. That helped my decision, too. I didn't want to go to New York and so that was why I was looking for something.

Ironically enough and I guess it can be told now, I really wasn't that interested in the fire department. I was making thirty-three hundred dollars working for the Federal government and, of course, to take the fire department job I had to take a cut to twenty-four hundred dollars which was a lot of money in those days. My fiancé's father was on the police department in Newark. And of course they all remembered the great time in the depression when the police and firemen all worked. I think they always thought there would be another depression every five or ten or fifteen years. They were looking for security for their daughter and really my mother-in-law, future mother-in-law at the time, sent the application in for me. I was astonished when I got the notice to appear for the test. That's really what did it.

Vesey: I wanted a steady job. (Laughter)

McCormack: I guess I became a firefighter by accident. I knew someone who had a relative who was a firefighter. I didn't know the fellow, but the person I knew was taking the test because his relative was a firefighter and he gave me the application. And I took the test. I grew up during the depression being aware that civil service people were working while a lot of other people weren't. But that's not what motivated me to take the job at all. I took the test because this friend of mine was taking it. He asked me to take it with him and I took it. And I got appointed and I figured I'd try it and see what happens.

Masterson: My father was a fireman to start with and I guess I got the incentive from him talking to me and telling me to try out for the job.

Baldino: I never dreamed of becoming a firefighter. It was a coincidence and the timing that helped me decide. Captain Juliano, who is a very good friend of mine, came to visit one evening and told me about getting an application and giving it a try. He got me the application and stayed until I filled it out. He said there was a great need for firefighters at that time and if I passed I would probably be called very soon. The written test was on a Saturday afternoon. I worked a half day every Saturday, so I didn't lose any time off from work. At that time money was scarce and we couldn't afford to leave work for any reason other than sickness. As luck would have it the physical was also on a Saturday afternoon. I filed in July of 1951 and was sworn in October of 1951. If the test had been during the week, I would never have been a firefighter. I couldn't afford to take the time off. Talk about luck.

Deutch: I had no idea I would be a fireman as a young fellow. My dad would have made a good fireman because he chased all the fire engines in New York City. He'd be out all night chasing them and he never became a fireman. But I guess I took the job because of my friends. They were all firemen. That's the main reason.

Griffith: Basically, why I took the job originally was security. My father had been a Newark policeman for thirty years. I think at that particular time, not only in my home, but in a lot of homes, the trend was civil service security and things of that nature. That's what was talked about. When the chance came up, my father mentioned it to me. We followed through on it and I was fortunate enough to be appointed provisional. But security was really the big reason I took the job. I was only twenty-four, but I always knew that somewhere down the line a pension and all those other things that went along with it were going to be important. Now at sixty-two I realize that it was a really good move for me anyway

Wall: Because I needed a job. Maybe I'm unusual, but we have no history of either police or fire in my family. Now, I came out of the military in 1952 and the economy wasn't so hot at the time. I went to work for the Department of the Army in Kearny and a co-worker was taking the exam. He convinced me to take it. At that time we took both the police and fire at the same time. Took more cops than they took fire, so I was appointed to the police in January 1954. And in November 1954 my name came up on the fire list and I came over to fire.

Freeman: Well, I took a chance. When I got out of the Navy I had a few odd jobs. Everybody worked for Bamberger's and so did I. Then after that I worked down neck at a place called Bart Smelting. In the interim I joined the auxiliaries. I lived across the street from Twelve Engine on Belmont Avenue. I just thought it was exciting. I like exciting things. So anyway, I was over there and a test came up. In fact I was assigned to Five Truck. One of the guys there talked me into taking the exam. I didn't want to take the exam because I wanted to go to Newark College of Engineering; it's now NJIT, to get a degree in electrical engineering. I was really interested in that. I said, "No, I don't want to be a fireman." That wasn't the kind of job I want. I wanted a white-collar job. Eventually they said, "Well, you can always take the test. Then once you get your degree and everything, you can quit the job and do whatever you want." I did take the exam and I came out pretty high. In fact, I think I came out number five or maybe I was number two, something like that. I took the job and I'm still here. I like it.

McGee: Well, I had just recently gotten discharged from the service and I was going from job to job. A couple of friends in our group had joined various fire departments and thought it was a good idea. I took the entrance test and was fortunate. I had no previous interest in firefighting or knew of anything about firemen. There is no fireman in my family. Most of my brothers and sisters are all professionals, lawyers and so on. So it was basically, at the right place at the right time and having come out of the service.

Stoffers: Well, the exam came up, is one reason. I always wanted to be a cop, but the exams didn't come up. I came out of the service and was working in a factory making intermediate frequency transformers for television sets. I didn't care for that too much, so I took a job in McCearn and Turny in Harrison as a machinist apprentice. That's where I met Tommy Gervel. He was an apprentice, too. I was there for a couple of years. Then an opening came up on the Police Department switch board. So, I was able to get that job temporarily. I think I started that job in May of '56. I was waiting on the fire department.

McGrory: Well, I was working in Otis elevator from the time I got out of the Army. I was in Otis elevator before I got into the Army. When I came out, things had changed in the number of years I was in the service and I got disillusioned. I saw I wasn't going anyplace. I saw a few of my friends and acquaintances in the area I lived in Newark, in Vailsburg, were either fireman or cops. Somebody got me an application and I took the test for fire department.

I never wanted to be a cop. I don't know why. I took the test for the fire department. I just took it. I didn't prepare for it. I didn't do anything, not really meaning to take the job. Then after I took the test, they published the test and I found out where I was. Now I'm waiting because I want to get out of Otis. Otis was a good company to work for a few years before that. Then it started to change. I was an expediter, which was not a bad job, but I couldn't see myself doing very much more there. So, when I did get appointed, I was happy to get appointed. I got appointed in June of 1957 and was very happy to hear of it because from that January to June I was dying to get out of Otis. The fire department was new to me. Nobody in the family had any connection with the fire department except for an uncle who was a volunteer fireman in East Newark.

Denvir: Back in1958, I was working for Public Service. At the time they were downsizing. I was laid off and went to work at TWA. In the mean time, the test for the job came up, so I took it with a few friends. I figured it was a good job. It was mainly security. I was looking for something steady. I never gave it too much thought. I did a little bit of forest firefighting when I was in the service. That was something. We had a little training. I did know a few people on the job, but they just said, "You might as well take it." The test was there so I just took it.

Freda: Well, believe it or not, I never really had a burning desire to be a fireman. Nor did I give it much thought until I was discharged from the service at an early age. In fact, I was only nineteen years old and I was a disabled veteran. That played a part in me accepting the job. And I was starting to get serious with a girl. I was thinking of marriage and I started thinking of employment. As luck would have it, the fire department had an entrance test. To add to that, I had disabled veteran status, which would help me on any civil service test. I was young and I wasn't that ambitious. It just made it easy for me.

So I took the fire department test with the premise that people in those days were security conscious. Security type jobs meant more than going out and getting a job with a large salary. That was the thinking. So we put these things all together, that's why I accepted the job. I had no idea what the job was. I didn't know what I was getting into. I never thought of that. The old scenario of those people who grow up and want to be a hero, a firefighter, none of these things entered it. I just took the job because it was a job and it was very convenient for me at the time, plus the security angle.

Charpentier: Well, I always wanted to be a fireman. My father was a fireman for about thirty- nine years. I liked the work. Before I was on I belong to the Bell and Siren, the fire auxiliary, and it just appealed to me. I was a cop for almost three years. The only reason I went there was because the job I was doing was driving a bus. The guy was going bankrupt so I took both exams. In fact, it was the same day. I took the both exams and the police came up first because at that time they were considering putting a fourth tour on and they didn't have enough men on the list. They had to get what they called a quickie list behind it to get enough men for the forty-two hour week, so we were held up, oh, maybe three years. I knew it was a secure job. My father was a fireman and my grandfather before him was a cop.

Marcell: I don't know. I was looking for a steady job. I was working laying bricks. I went up to West Side High School and took the test. They had three tests, State Trooper, a fireman, and a cop. I passed the State Trooper and the firemen and I passed what I thought was the cop's exam, but I waited about three weeks. I got a letter in the mail from civil service saying I came out number one on the list. And I said, "Jesus." It said we go up to Vailsburg High School with blue jeans and a shirt. I went up there and I brought the application with me. They said, "When can you start work?" I said, "Gees, there can't even be time to buy a uniform and stuff." She said, "A uniform and stuff?" I said, "Yes." She said, "You just passed the custodian's test." I was going to be a janitor for there. (Laughter)

No, I took the test down in Barringer High School. I took the State Trooper's test before and I was waiting for them to call. The Fire Department called me first. I came on the job and I went up to Eleven Engine. Right after that about a month, two months later the State Police called me. I went down and they said I had to stay five days a week and you got two days off or something like that. I was just married and my wife and I had a little kid. I couldn't do that, so I stayed on the fire department job. But it's the best job I ever had in my life. I would never change it for anything else. Believe me when I say that. So, that's why I took the fireman's test. It was a steady job.

Smith: When I got out of the Army, I was employed as a warehouse man. This was in the mid-'50s. Things started to wind down economically and I was laid off, re-hired, laid off. Then somebody said, "Well, let's take the police and fire department tests." I took both. I had a member of my family years back who was a Newark fireman. He took it during the depression. They were never laid off, but the city paid them in script. If that was the case, then I'll take it. I was called by the police department first; I was talked out of that; and then I took the fire department job.

Miller: Well, the main reason was when I was about ten, eleven years old I lived right around the corner from the firehouse, Seven Engine. I went to school at Saint Joseph's. Hanging out there, talking to some of the old timers, and encouragement from my father that civil service would always be a steady job, although not the most rich and lucrative job in the world. You'd always have something to eat. Also several other people who went to Saint Joseph's became firemen. I could name maybe ten others who were all from the neighborhood. I don't know if they were influenced for reasons that I was, but basically that's why I became a fireman.

Dunn: Why did I become a firefighter? Probably a quack of fate, I was always interested. When I was a very young boy, I lived down neck. I moved into a house across the street from Eight Truck and Sixteen Engine. At the beginning of my first school year, going to kindergarten, I was always infatuated with the firehouse across the street. I never quite got to kindergarten because I would spend the mornings in the firehouse. I became their little mascot.

At the time it was just elderly men in the fire companies because it was during World War II. There were no young firemen. They worked extremely long shifts. So, every morning I would go out to go to school, Hawkins Street School. I'd cross Ferry Street with my mother and she'd leave me on the corner. I'd walk down and make a right hand turn into Eight Truck and I'd sit there until kindergarten was over. Then I'd walk home. I guess that was my beginning experience of the Fire Department. So I can't say the Fire Department was a security blanket type of job as I grew older or a salary job. It was just a job I always perceived that I would like to do.

When went into high school I took testing for what you would like to be when you grow up. I always tested to be a social worker. I tried to always explain to the teacher, "You're misguiding thought of a social worker is someone working for welfare." I was always interested in doing good for the people of the city and I always had in the back of my mind the fire service in that context. So even though the profile exam I was taking was for social worker, I really perceived the Fire Department to be a social type of job. After high school I entered the Marine Corps. When I came out of the Marine Corps I got a job in Clinton Auto Square. But I always had the idea of a job with some type of security and getting a better type of job and the fire exam came along.

Both my brother and I went up to take the test. I was fortunate and I passed the examination. My brother didn't. Then I waited for the appointment. When this testing took place it was for the forty-two hours being instituted in the fire department. There was a large number being employed. What really surprised me was that the fire car went up and down the street giving out notices to the people coming on the job and they never came to my house. What I didn't know was that there were two lists at the time and I was on the second list. So I was very upset and when the forty-two hour class went on and I didn't get my card I became very upset. I wanted to find out why. That's the first time I preceded to ask a politician on the street "How come I'm not a fireman?" and I got the information.

Fortunately for me six people didn't show up for the swearing in of the forty-two hours. So the firemen you will interview who came on with the forty-two hours all started March first. I was hired six weeks later. It was April ninth. We replaced the six people who didn't show up. I was one of the guys who replaced them. Every time I have trouble in the Fire Department I always blame it on when I went through the Fire Academy. I only had half the time because everyone had six weeks and I only had two weeks.

Belzger: Times were tough. I needed a job. That's really the truth. I'd just come out of the Navy and I was working on fire extinguishers with my dad, who was at that time on Palm Street, Twenty-six Engine. It was a family tradition also. My grandfather was a fireman. He started in 1912 in Seventeen Engine. That's when they had horses there. It's ironic because I ended up in Seventeen Engine. I was used to the firehouse because dad worked in Five Truck. I used to go down there quiet often.

Carragher: For security, before I came on the fire department, I was a union carpenter. I was an assistant foreman in a wood working shop. Every year come the winter with the snow or something like that, you'd probably get a lay off for a week or two. But I didn't get the lay off. I was single and didn't get laid off because I was assistant foreman. Married guys were getting laid off. I guess around 1958, we had quite a bit of snow there and the guys lost quite a bit of time. I didn't lose any. I was still there and they all came in yelling and screaming, "You should take the time, not us. We're married. We need the money." I said, "Hey, I need money, too. Just because I'm single, doesn't mean you don't need money." So, I guess I came home and it started bothering me a little bit.

This was going into early 1959, I guess or late in 1958. I read the paper where the Newark Fire Department wanted to hire people for the fire department. They were going to a forty-two hour shift. So, I thought to myself, "Well, let me try it." Prior to this I thought a fireman's job or a cop's job was for lazy people. Who the hell wants those jobs? But I decided I'd try the test. I took the test and got on the list. I got hired and liked the job from day one.

Harris: To tell you the truth, I became a fireman for the simple reason that the job I was working at, I was working as an assistant shipping clerk, the company was moving out of state and wasn't taking anybody with them. What I did, I took four exams, police, fire, postal, and correction officer. That's the first one to call. Because I knew it also had security to it and I was basically just starting my family.

Haran: Well, actually what had happened with me was when I graduated from high school in '56; I went to work for the telephone company, known as New Jersey Bell at that time. My father had worked there. My mother worked there. I had two sisters who worked there and my brother Jack worked there. So, it was more or less expected of me to go to work with the telephone company, which I did. After eleven months with the telephone company, they had their first lay off ever in the history of New Jersey Bell. They laid off everybody under a year's service. I had eleven months on the job.

I was born and raised in the City of Newark, attended parochial schools in Newark. I grew up in a neighborhood that had all cops and firemen. It seemed that every other house was a cop or a fireman. When I was laid off from the phone company, I was talking to guys. They said, "Hey, what are you going to do now that you're laid off? Why don't you take a test for the fire department or the police department?" I knew a lot of people in the police and fire departments. So that's what I did. I didn't have anything lined up when I got laid off. There was a test coming up for the fire department. I took the test, but I prepared for the test.

They used to give courses in some of the firehouses back then. Chief Nolen was a Captain of Six Truck. There was myself and Angelo Ricca, who rose to the rank of Deputy Chief. We all were taking these courses to study for the entrance exam to come on the fire department. We used to go down to Six Truck a couple of nights a week when Captain Nolen was working. We would go over old tests and he'd prepare us for the entrance examination. At that time the fire department was changing their schedule from fifty-six hours a week to forty-two hours a week and the job became very attractive to a lot of men. Not only that, a lot of fellows had just come home from Korea. They were looking for work.

I knew it was going to be difficult for me to get this job because veterans had preference and I wasn't a veteran. That's why I went down and studied. They had the exam. As a result I came out two hundred and thirty seventh on the list. I was the twelfth or thirteenth non-veteran. They started putting the first fellows on the list on March 1, 1959. I believe we took the test somewhere around September or October. We weren't notified until sometime in February I believe of '59 whether you passed the test or not. They put you on an eligibility list.

I think the first fifteen guys were disabled veterans. Then I believe there were approximately two hundred veterans after that and then ten or twelve of us who were non-veterans. As a result of not being a veteran, I didn't get appointed to the job until December 4, 1961, which was almost three years later. The list was running out. Actually, the list did run out. The list was a two-year list. I kept calling Civil Service up all the time. In the mean time I had been hired back with the phone company, but now I had made up my mind that I wanted to be a fireman. I had talked myself into it and other people had talked me into it. So, I kept calling Civil Service up to find out where I was on the list. Was I approaching the magic number to get appointed to the job? Two years was coming up and the list ran out. They extended it for six months. I didn't get called in that six-month time either, so they extended it for another six months. I believe around the third month of the second six-month extension, they hired five guys. I was one of them. We were the last five guys taken off that list. That was December 4, 1961. I was appointed to the job.

I honestly feel if I hadn't gone down to Six Truck with Captain Nolen at that time and studied for the entrance exam, I wouldn't have had extra questions that I picked up from him down in the firehouse. I attributed my entrance into the Newark Fire Department based on Captain Nolen.

Butler: I thought it's an interesting career. It would be a career that offered definite job security, which later turned out to be a farce. But in the time that I was looking in the late '50s, early '60s it definitely offered a steady job without possibility of closing down or laying off.

I felt that not only did it have good job security, but eventually it'd be a good salary. I would be doing something worthwhile instead of mundane or ho-hum office job or assembly line job. That it would be something worthwhile. It did happen later on that I was involved in a few rescues and it did make me feel that I was able to give something to the city.

Cahill: Well, because somebody told me it was a good job and it had security. I knew a couple of guys on the job, nobody from the family, nothing like that. There was an Irvington Fire Captain where I worked who really just kind of talked me into taking the exam, taking the job.

Highsmith: Well, I became a fireman just by chance. I happened to meet a young man by the name of John Coxton. He was on the fire department. He worked at Five Truck. At the time, I was going to take the policeman's exam. John Coxton came and sat down at my house. He talked to me. He said, "You know, you work two days on, you get one day off. You work two nights on, you get three days off." And so what he was saying about the fire department was very inviting. He didn't tell me about any dangers or anything. So I crossed out police department and put down fire department. And that's how I became a fireman.

Cody: I was first introduced to the fire department when I was in the Air Force. I was assigned to the Air Force fire department crash rescue and structural. When I came out, it seemed like very good job in the Air Force, so I figured it had to be a pretty good job in civilian life. When I came out of the service, I got a job driving a bus for Public Service, which is now New Jersey Transit. I used to drive the bus that passed Eight Engine and a friend of mine used to always be sitting out there reading his paper. As I drove by I used to stop and talk to him for a minute. I said "Gees, why am I driving this bus when I can be doing that?" On a lark, a couple of us from the bus company got the applications; took the test; and here I am. I had no desire ever or even thought of being a fireman as I was growing up.

Garrity: When I was a kid, my father was a provisional fireman in Harrison during the Second World War. One particular Saturday there had been a Friday night-Saturday morning fire. He and I walked down to this fire, which was about ten blocks from our house. When we got there they were just taking up the hose from the last engine company. The Captain of that company was a very good friend of not only my father, but my family.

He said to my father, "Why don't you put him on the engine and we'll drive him back to the firehouse." That's when I decided wanted to be a fireman. That's a true story. That actually happened.

Knight: First off, my father was a Fire Captain from 1942 to 1959. He was killed, not on the job, but it was job related. It was something I always wanted to do. I wanted to be a fireman since I was a little kid. I enjoyed the work. I took the job primarily for the security, because back in the early '60's jobs were cheap and you were always getting laid off from one thing or another. With civil service you were always secure on your job. You knew you weren't going to get laid off and that your job was going to be there everyday. You would be drawing a paycheck every two weeks.

Wargo: Security. I was on another job, but nothing seemed as secure as a civil service job at the time. The salary was about the same. There wasn't much difference in that. When I was in the Navy I saw firefighters on the base in the Navy and thought I would like to do that type of job when I got out. It sort of slipped away from me for a year or two and then I ran into a few firemen. They explained the job to me. Another reason I took it was because of the time off during the week, the shifts. I liked being off three days in a row.

McGovern: Other than what I learned in the Navy, I knew nothing about firefighting when I came on. I went to firefighting school in the Navy and damage control, but I never had any childhood ambition to be a fireman. I got out of the Navy and went to work for Western Electric and I hated it, couldn't stand it. My cousin who was on the job, Donny McCormick, he told me the test was coming up for fireman. So, I took the test and I came out fourteenth. It just happened to work out that way. As a matter of fact I think there were two tests. There was a telegraph lineman's test coming up at the same time and the firemen's test came first. Within three to four months they called and I left Western Electric. That was thirty-three years ago.

D. Prachar: Why I became a firefighter? It's a family tradition, having a great grandfather who was killed on the job. My grandfather was a member of Ten Engine, two uncles on the job, my brother on the job, myself, and now my nephew, which will be the fifth generation.

J. Cosby: Basically I became a firefighter for security reasons. The previous job I worked at was at the Ford Motor Company. It was an assembly line job and entailed a lot of layoffs and strikes. So, I wanted a more secure job. That's the reason I became a firefighter, although I was making more money at Ford Motor Company. But it didn't offer me the security of the fire department.

I would say too, that my oldest brother had a lot to do with it. It's what made me interested. He was a firefighter. He was the one who encouraged me to take the exam. I used to hang around the firehouse and watched how they worked and things he did. That sort of made me interested in the fire department, but I think the main reason was the security aspect of the job. I don't think a job can be more secure. I've been on the job twenty-two years and haven't missed a payday while working or being sick. I think that's pretty good security, although you don't make as much money as in private industry.

Finucan: Why did I become a firefighter? I became a firefighter because my father was a firefighter. I knew it was a good job. He was a Fire Captain in Newark for thirty-two years. He came on the job in 1947, retired in 1979. My uncle was also a firefighter. In fact I have a cousin who's in the academy right now.

Pianka: I had nothing better to do. I was in an office job. I just didn't like it. I happened to frequent this bar with Joe Lefchak and Eddy Jankowski. We were sitting and drinking one day. I told them, "I'm not happy with this job." And they said, "Hey, test is coming up. Why don't you take it?" I had no idea what I was getting into. Anyway, I took the test and anguished a little about taking it because I had no idea what was going on. I kept asking, "Can I do this job?" Because I knew they were big guys and I wasn't that big a guy. They said, "Don't worry about it. You'll do all right." Anyway the day came. I was appointed.

I'll never forget my first day going to the firehouse. I was on the fourth tour assigned to Five Truck on Belmont Avenue. I walked in the backyard and through the door. There's Danny McCoy, Captain McCoy. And Danny was shorter than me and twice my weight. I said, "If he can do it. I can do it."

McDonnell: I was going to college and I was working a full-time job at Westinghouse while I was going to school. I had actually taken the test in 1967 and I came out number one, but I didn't take the job. I was living with my brother-in-law. He was a fireman. I was living in the same house they were living in. I was going to school and I didn't know the hours they worked. My brother-in-law had always egged me to take the test. "Why don't you take the test?"

When I had taken it in '67, I was living on Broadway. I had no phone. I was going to school. I was working at night. I lived in Newark and my mother lived on Norwich. I used her address because she had a phone. By the time they got in touch with me it was too late. It was one of those real quick things. They notified you and the next day or two days later you were supposed to be getting sworn in. I didn't get the note. They slipped it under my door. I had to get it in that day. I called them up and told them who I was. I was supposed to be getting sworn in that afternoon. I was told, "We know about you." They probably figured I lived out of the city. I just turned it down. I took it again in '69. I was still going to school. It was my last year in school. I thought I would just take the job until I finished school.

I got the job. They notified me in May. I was just finishing up. I said let me go on and just take it and get a teaching job and that will be it. I'll leave, but I took the job, started in June. I went on June 1, 1970. I liked it, so instead of teaching I used to substitute a little. I used to substitute down at East Side High School. I liked the fire department. It was safer than being a teacher. I figured I'd stay on the fire department. It was paying the same. They had just gotten a raise after the strike the year before. So, I liked it. I liked that it was not routine. You never knew what you were going to do. Everyday coming to work was different. I didn't want to be that nine to five, steady rut kind of thing. Plus the hours you worked. You had lots of time off. I just stayed. That's how I became a fireman, unintentionally. It had nothing to do with the salary or security. I wasn't even thinking of that. My brother was a fireman. I had relatives on the Fire Department, but I really didn't have much of an interest in it.

Rotonda: Why did I become a fireman? Because somebody on the Seven Up truck told me, "Why don't you take the test?" I told him I couldn't afford this job and he said, "Take the test and then decide what you want to do." I took the job and I sweated making the money I lost. But it was the best move I ever made.

Melodick: Totally by accident. I had no incentive as far as being a fireman. A few of my friends came on this job, Myles McDonald, Pete Petrone, Chief Tansey. We all took the test the same day. At that time you were able to take both the police and fire test at the same time. They convinced me to take both. I happen to be called by the fire department first, which I thought never would have happened. I really despised the job I had at the time. My boss was a real jerk. I said, "I'll take the fire department and then I'll quit when the police department calls me." Well, I'll tell you what. Once I got in the firehouse I said, "No way, no way because this is the greatest job in the world." I was only on a short time and I knew how good it was. That's how it all started. It was an accident. The best accident I ever had in my life. It's the greatest job in the world.

T. Grehl: I graduated college in June of '71 and had a choice to either become a teacher or a fireman. I decided to become a fireman because I didn't want to sit behind a desk. I was still young and my father and grandfather were both firemen. I guess it was a little bit in my blood. My father told me "Stay five years and then move on." So, I decided not to take the teaching job and become a fireman. Thirty-one years later I'm still s fireman.

Ryan: Why did I become a fireman?   I have to think.   Why did I become a fireman?   Well, my first objective was to be a history teacher. Unfortunately, when I got out of service I was informed that there was a twelve year waiting period to become a history teacher as the educational field was flooded at the time.   The open statewide test came up.   I being a federal firefighter at the time was interested in a little bit of a raise and working thirty hours less a week.   So, I took the state wide test, came out number one on that, and was hired in November of 1973.

There was also a background of firefighting in our family.   My father, my uncle, my grandfather were all members of the Newark fire department. My grandfather went on the fire department I believe in about 1912.   His brother Patrick was a member of the police department.   He went on the police department I believe in 1896.   He was shot and killed in the line of duty in 1919.   My father was named after him and me after my father. Therefore we both share the same name only reversed.   My uncle was Patrick Joseph.   I'm Joseph Patrick.   I've enjoyed the career.   It's been tremendous to me.   I couldn't become a history teacher.   I had to go in some direction.   I was married and had two small children at home.

I did have an interest in the fire department.   When I got out of service in 1969, I immediately went to work for Bell Telephone.   The salary wasn't terrific.   The hours were very long.   My first year there I worked fourteen hundred hours overtime and still made less than I did the last year I was in service.   Opportunity came up.   I took a test for the federal fire department at Lakehurst Naval Air Station.   Passed that, was hired, and was promoted down there.   Unfortunately, we had a reduction in force and I was transferred to Fort Monmouth.   At the time I was at Fort Monmouth the state wide examination came up, the first and only offered in the state, but having been a Newark resident most of my life, it was a not that far a leap to come back to Newark.

My grandfather had a very interesting career in the fire department. He had been drafted from the fire department. His name is on the memorial as one of the members who were drafted into the Army for the First World War. Upon his return from the Army, because Uncle Patty was killed, he was placed in the Bureau of Combustibles. This was also the time of Prohibition. He was one of two members of the Bureau of Combustibles who were on what was known as the Whiskey Squad. Now you may ask what the Whiskey Squad is. During Prohibition the only way the that the police department could break into speak easies or illegal breweries or refineries or whatever they would be called was to have a fire inspector there who would say there's a flagrant fire violation in the building. They would break down the door and go in and alas there was a speakeasy or a brewery and the police would take over at that time. During the '30s he went back to Three Truck, was in Three Truck for most of the '30s. During the Second World War because of the manpower shortage, he again went back the Bureau of Combustibles and was in charge of the dock area. He was personal aide to Public Safety Director John B. Keenan and he retired in 1957. My family lived in Vailsburg just about our entire length of the time of service to the city. It's now over a hundred years of family service to the city of Newark.

Carter: Ever since I was a little kid I wanted to be a fireman. When the 1935 city service ladder truck used to rumble through downtown Freehold, I just got so excited. I wanted to be a part of it and I could never be a part of it because back then when I lived in Freehold Township. I couldn't be a member of the Freehold Fire Department. It was limited to the Borough residents only, not the Township, which was a separate municipality. So that led me to join the first aid squad, which led me to come home from college on weekends to be with the first aid squad, which lead me to flunk out of college. That led me to the Air Force fire department, which is a funny story. My parents were really mad at me for flunking out of an Ivy League school, so I went to join the Air Force because I didn't feel like carrying a rifle in Vietnam at the time.

I'm sitting there in the recruiters office thumbing through the book and he's giving me the old "What do you want to be, kid?" routine. I just happen to turn the page and saw a fire truck. I said, "I always wanted to be a fireman." I did four years in Alaska, the Philippines, and Vietnam, got out of the service and wanted to be a fireman. Having discovered that I loved being a fireman, but hated the Air Force, got an address in Asbury Park because you couldn't be a fireman unless you lived in a town in New Jersey. I flunked the test there because of the last exercise in the physical.

I used to ride with Jersey City Fire Department as a buff just to go to fires. Joined the volunteers at home and then I guess it was 1972 along about April, I was riding with Jersey City, bemoaning the fact that I couldn't be a fireman like I wanted to be. I was driving a school bus, which told me my original plans for being a business education teacher were worthless because I couldn't stand the kids. I'm in the firehouse and this guy Johnny from Engine Four said, "Well, I got just the ticket for you. They just changed the law. Here." I filed for first statewide offering. I filed for all that I could check off and came out first on the list in Carteret, second in Rahway, second in Plainfield. July fifth I got the phone call from Rahway. July sixth I went for the interview. They said, "When can you start?" I said, "Well, I got my gear in the car." I started that day. Then I started buffing in Newark because I wanted to get a little experience and go to some fires.

Well, I became very impressed with the difference between the Rahway Fire Department and the Newark Fire Department.

In Rahway I was a janitor who rode on fire trucks very infrequently. When I went to Newark, I went to fires. And even though I was an auxiliary, the chief of that battalion at the time, Chief Reheis, knew I was a trained fireman for another town. I got away with stuff nobody else ever got away with. I mean like when they were riding one and two and I was there he considered the company to be one and three. The only thing he wouldn't let me do was roofs, because he knew I was clumsy.

But I would literally leave home, because the Rahway schedule was three on, three off, three on, three off, days, nights, days, come up for my first night and I'd go night Rahway, all day Newark, night Rahway, all day Newark. That's back in the early '70s when there were fires pretty much any time you came up. I'm saying to myself, "I love being a fireman, but in Rahway I don't do anything but clean fire trucks, cut the grass, do windows and in Newark there was this overwhelming lack of, for want of a better phrase, bullshit tasks to do.

One day Chief Reheis came into the fire house, I believe it was a Friday and he said, "Harry I got something for you. The applications for Newark are out." Now this is back in the days when everything counted, earliest post mark, everything. I just happened to have my veterans preference number in my pocket, because I'd been filing for a lot of other towns to get out of Rahway. And zoomed down to the Post Office and filed the day that I got the application, which is the day the applications came out.

Langenbach: Oh, that's a good question. I came out of the Peace Corps and I was married. We had a baby on the way. I was working for a plumber. I hated the job. I was working nights as a bartender. My father-in-law worked for the Star Ledger and he saw an ad in there for the Newark Fire Department. He said, "You gotta to do something to take care of my daughter better than what you're doing, so you can take this job." So, that's why I took the test. It was a hint from my father-in-law that you better do something better than working as a plumber and tending bar all night.

My dad was a cop, so I was leaning that way when I got out of the service and he said absolutely not. He said, "If you become a cop, I'll shoot you." The Fire Department interested me. I make light of it, but it was more once I got involved. I took the test and I really got into it. Yes, I'm glad I did.

Luxton: I really don't know. I had a friend who was a volunteer in Nutley. He talked me into being a volunteer fireman. I enjoyed it. It was fun. I had just come out of the Navy and I was looking for excitement or whatever, a chance to break windows. I didn't have much of a job and the guy who did the fire alarm work in Nutley passed away. My future father-in-law came up to me and said, "If you don't go after that job you're nuts." because I was doing fire alarm work. I thought about it. Yes, it's probably not a bad idea, so I went after the job. Then I had difficulty because I had hernia. They weren't too sure whether it was or whether it wasn't a hernia. So that knocked me out of the box. I was on temporary. This was the entrance exam. In the mean time, I had taken a couple of other tests to prepare for it. I had taken one in Passaic. I took one in Paterson. At the time, you didn't have to be a city resident.

I went to a doctor about the hernia and they said, "Well, let's just do an operation and find out for sure." They cut me open and I did have a minor hernia. I got in touch with the civil service commissioner and they were able to take my Passaic physical test and put it in combination my Nutley written and physical performance. That got me number 1A on the Nutley list. I ended up taking that job. I guess I had it for about a year. It was the assistant alarm superintendent's job. Then when there was about eleven months to go, they called for a test. Somebody didn't like the fact that I was going to beat everybody else. They wrangled it so the test was called when I had eleven months, three weeks, five days on the job. I didn't have the year. I got bounced off of that and into the regular firefighting field.

Nutley had two companies, an engine and a truck, and thirty paid guys. Two fire officers and seven guys on a tour. I worked there for a while and I got bored. There wasn't a lot to do. I don't think they counted runs then. We must have been maybe doing five or seven hundred, something like that. It wasn't a lot. Then the opportunity came for the Newark test. There were three or four of us from Nutley who took it. It seemed like the thing to do. I was probably twenty-four or twenty-five, something like that. It had just opened up to eighteen year olds.

That's when the mutual aid law was signed, where people could move out of the city. Because they could move out of the city, they had a mutual aid pact, so you didn't have to worry about the recall and so forth. So, the test was opened to state wide. Thirty-seven or thirty-eight hundred people took the test and I came out number two. I think I am one of the few veterans in the city of Newark who lost ground because of veterans' preference. I had veterans' preference, but there were six disabled vets in front of me so I ended up being number seven.

Connell: I guess it all started when I was about nine or ten years old. There was a large bowling alley about a block and a half down the street from me. One night it caught fire. I ran down about twelve o'clock at night and watched the fire. I was just impressed by it. Always wondered what it would look like inside a burning building. It was always in the back of my mind.

I never really thought too much about it until after I got out of the service. I was working in a manufacturing place where they made florescent ballasts and at night I was bartending in a neighborhood bar. One of the guys who came in was a fireman and I got pretty friendly with him. He kept on asking me, "How come you're not a fireman?" "Well, I never knew how to go about it. I always thought it was political." He turned me on to the applications. It just fell into place and I've loved it ever since.

Pignato: I became a fireman because they called before the Police Department. I was a Long Branch volunteer fireman. To become a volunteer fireman they suggested I should take the test for the Newark Fire Department. Study with the guys who really wanted to be Newark firemen and I'll learn something. Since I just started as a volunteer fireman, I said, "I'll try it." I took the test and came out ahead of all the other guys who took the test. I decided to take the job. The Captain at Three Truck at the time talked me into taking the job. He lived in my area and explained to me it was such a great job, all the camaraderie and all the other things I was looking for in a job, so I took it.

Perdon: In all honesty, it was a better job than what I was doing and I was surrounded by firemen. Tommy Jones from Five Truck on the first tour got me the application. Made sure I took the test.

Langevin: Salary and security, but prior to becoming a firefighter I worked for New Jersey Bell Telephone. I wasn't real happy with the job. I wanted a little bit better salary and some better benefits. I took the firefighter test and came out very well. That was the only statewide test ever given in the city. And I came out pretty high, so I decided to take the job. I've never looked back.

Ricca: Part tradition in the family, part wanting to help people. Definitely wasn't the pay because the pay was lower than what I was making back when I started. I left a pretty good job doing air conditioning refrigeration for Food Fair, Pantry Pride stores and I took the fire department test. My brothers were a big influence, Angelo probably more than Joe. Angelo was fifteen years older than me. I was always the baby to him even though we had a younger sister. He tried to talk me into becoming a cadet. Then when I saw the application with five thousand dollars on it, I said I just couldn't do it because I had just bought a new car. I was going down the shore every week end. He said, "Take it." He said, "You study, you'll do good. It will be a career for you." I didn't even take the cadet test. For some reason or other I think Joe brought the application home for the regular test, sometime right after the cadet program started. And I took it on a lark. Joe said, "Take it. If you come out good, you take the job. If not, you don't. Nothing lost if you don't want the job." That was the input from the family.

Gesualdo: Desperation. In the mid-'70s, there was no other work around. I was a disabled vet at the time. I still am, but I had to use my disabled vet status to find employment. After ten years with Public Service Electric and Gas as a lineman, I left there to go to England with my wife for a year and a half. That was in '75. Came back in '77 and there was no work around. So, I figured take the civil service test. I was a firefighter in England for a year and a half, so it was kind of in my blood at that point.

So, I just applied to all the fire departments where I could take the test and Newark was the first one that had openings.

Chapter Three: Entrance Test

Fredette: Originally we took the exam in 1938. That was why we were able to get in. There were about fifteen of us who were in our early thirties when we got appointed. At that time firemen had to be under thirty and a policeman had to be between twenty-five and thirty-one. A fireman had to be between twenty-one and thirty. That was the age limit when you filed, not when you took the examination.

I passed the physical. I passed the medical. You see, if not for the war years, the doctors would have knocked me down. I was around ninety-sixth on my written test, coming in. I wound up with an 80.9 on the entrance. They just gave me a seventy on the physical and a seventy on the medical because I got crushed under a horse wagon back around 1930. I drove a team of horses for the Ford Motor Company back in '27, '28, '29, and '30. The iron handle went right through my stomach. When I stripped down they saw this big eighteen-inch gash in my stomach. They just gave me that. In the war years they were looking for men. Outside the scar on my stomach, I looked okay. They were glad to get able-bodied men for the fire department.

When we took the examination, you had to have so many of your own teeth; take the plates out. No glasses. Flat feet, they would knock you down for flat feet. Some of the guys got away with the plates. Like one guy, his father was the Police Commissioner. There was another family whose uncles were captains. The father was a Battalion Chief. They were always in politically. They got in. They didn't have to take any plates out. But other guys, if you didn't know anybody, you took it out. You had to be a certain height and a certain weight. If you were overweight they would knock you down.

I remember one guy, he worked for Ward Bakery, he used to get out early in the morning and run around West Side Park to try and lose five pounds. He couldn't make it. He was just a solid built man; that was all there was to it. They knocked him down. I think he really could have been a good fireman because he was very interested in the job. Anybody who would run in West Side Park early in the morning before he took a bread route out just to make the job had to want to be a fireman real bad.

Vetrini: A written test, a hundred questions. We had some multiple-choice questions and some true and false. You took an agility test with push-ups, climbed a rope, and the medical thing.

Redden: It was a hundred true and false, might have been a hundred and twenty-five, and the test was for both police and fire. It was one test for both departments. When the list came out, I wasn't high enough on it to go with the first group. The first group taken off it went on the police department. Then the next group, which I was in, went on the fire department. I believe there had to be over a hundred of us that went on the fire department, all veterans from World War II.

Kinnear: The type of test we took was a written test and then a physical test. The physical consisted of push-ups, sit-ups. The written was a multiple choice as I recall it.

Masters: In my day it had a lot of hydraulics to it, math and all that, and then general questions. The physical was held at Sussex Avenue Armory on Sussex Avenue. It's gone now. The building's gone. Our physical was climbing the rope, lifting weights, and stuff like that. We had to go through a barrel about fifty feet long. I guess to see if you're not afraid of crawling in the dark.

F. Grehl: At that time it was a true and false test of pretty close to a hundred to a hundred and twenty-five questions in which there was a penalty. For every true question you got one right, for every false question you didn't get one wrong, you got two wrong. You were basically penalized for guessing. So if you got one wrong, you lost an extra point. If you didn't answer it you just lost one point. It was a more competitive examination. Basically, the examination was on the civics, math, English, civics of Newark, and geography. One of the stupidest questions was, "Which is the longest street in the City of Newark?" I had no idea which one that was. It's Raymond Boulevard.

There was a physical very, very similar to the one that they had for promotional exams at the time which was push-ups, sit-ups, vertical rope climb, vertical jump, long jump, and those Russian squats. That's basically what the physical was. We also had to run a bag down. There was no obstacle course, just run it down around a circle and back. Your scores on the two of them were put together and you got an entrance mark. Although there was competition to get on a little earlier with the first twenty instead of the second twenty because you picked up seniority, the lists were all cleaned off. Within six to eight months they just put everybody on because they needed them so bad.

Vesey: It was general, general knowledge. I took the test for the police and fire, separate times. You took the written and later you were notified for the physical. It wasn't right away. It was three or four months, maybe longer than that. I came out almost even on both tests.

Masterson: We had a written and a physical. You had to pass the written, the physical, and then a medical later on. Then you had another medical with Doctor Tenore, who was the department surgeon. The physical was with the pushups and the sit ups and all that. Police and fire physicals were the same. The written tests were different. When you were down at the armory taking the physical, it was for either police or fire. It made no difference because they were both the same and they marked you up. There were forty-two push-ups, sixty-five squat jumps, and if I remember right you had to climb a rope, straight up a rope. Broad jump, I think they had that in there, sit-ups, push-ups, and then they had eye tests. They'd give you eye tests down there. The doctor would check you for eyes and flat feet and stuff like that. The surgeon used to check you again. Your eyes had to be twenty/twenty in both eyes at that time. That was a tricky one. That was a "get you."

Deutch: It was a general knowledge test with a lot of automotive questions and State questions. I think I did very well because of the mechanical questions on the exam. Some of the questions were true and false and a lot of questions were on the State government. There was a good physical. We took our physical in Elizabeth and I was in very good shape. After that my legs felt it. I was worn out from some of the exercises you did.

Wall: It was a general intelligence test as I recall, plus the physical. I think we took the one exam in the morning and the other exam in the afternoon.

Freeman: The written was more or less like an intelligence test. There was nothing fire department about it. I think it was math, English, and reading comprehension. That was about it. And you took a physical where you had to do pushups. You had to do a vertical jump along a wall to see how high you could jump. You would stand next to a wall. They'd give you a piece of chalk and you would just squat down and see how high you could jump. I think you got two chances. Then they would measure where you put the mark. You had to do so many sit-ups. Everything was timed except the vertical jump. There was a timed run doing something. Then there was a back pull. There was a big round meter with a needle on it and a place on the bottom where you could put your feet. You would stand on it. Then there was a chain with a handle and you'd pull. A back pull, I think they called it. What you'd do is keep your feet straight and then you would just straighten up and pull as hard as you could up. That needle would go across and it would stop. That was the extent of the physical.

McGee: As I remember it was pretty easy actually. It was a general knowledge test, not firefighting. They would ask you civic questions. Who was your governor? How many senators you have? General information, I guess they were looking for some grounded people, people who have a little knowledge of everything rather than focused on any one particular area. The physical portion was harder than the physical portion today. You had to climb a rope eighteen feet in a gym hand over hand; had to do so many push-ups and so many sit-ups. And the last one was the Russian kazatskies, which were very hard on the knees. Most people couldn't walk down the stairs when they got done, but as it is today, most guys are in pretty good shape and they did very, very well. There was also a different rating between the written and the physical, in the scoring of the test. I think it might have been like an eight and two. It seemed to be the emphasis was on a lot on general knowledge plus the physical, but everybody did well in the physical.

Denvir: It was a general knowledge of everything. You had to know the wheels and different kinds of tools. If you knew what they were and did a little arithmetic, some basic English, and a little reading comprehension, you did well. You also had to take a physical. At that time they had the back pull, sit-ups, the run with the bag, climbed a rope up and down, and squat jumps. That was the last thing you did, the squat jumps.

Marcell: It was a regular written test, a little bit of everything and then a physical, too.

Miller: Well, it was a lot harder than it is today. I think it was more like a general IQ test. It involved about a hundred and twenty five questions in maybe two or three hours. The criteria were math, English, physics, tools, and equipment. It was a well-rounded test that you had to know a little bit about. There were some things that I didn't know. I can recall just one of the test questions at the time because I wasn't into tools and they wanted to know what a star tool was. I had gotten it right just by guessing, but that stuck in my mind at the time. I thought it was a very fair test. I didn't do that tremendously well on it. I don't think anybody did. I think I got in maybe the high seventies on the written part. I came out like a hundred and thirty six on the entrance class out of three hundred and some odd people. But of the hundred and thirty six, I think a hundred and twenty in front of me were veterans. I wasn't a veteran. So, in that respect I did pretty well. I guess I held my own.

Of course, there was a physical that went along with it. The physical consisted of push-ups, sit-ups, squats, running with a dummy, high jump, climbing the rope, and a hand squeeze, where you had to squeeze your hand. The most difficult was climbing the rope. You had to go up from a sitting position all the way to the top of the Elizabeth armory, touch the main rafter, and come down. That would give you a hundred. It was difficult for the heavier guys, but lighter, thin guys could make it up to the top and get a hundred on that. I did get a pretty good physical, in the nineties. But then you had your combined scores. I think I took that exam in 1957 and I didn't get on the job until 1959. You had to wait two years until the list was promulgated and they started putting people on.

Smith: The test I took, to me, was nothing more than a general high school review, with a smattering of events. If you read the newspaper every day, you wouldn't be at a loss. The physical consisted of so many squat jumps, sit-ups. You had to climb a rope. You had to run and then carry a two hundred pound duffle bag any way you could from position "A" to position "B". Then you had a medical. That was it. Most of the men there were in their late twenties or middle twenties. There was nobody any younger than that because at that time, you couldn't get the job unless you were a veteran. Not because they made it that way, that's just the way it fell. Somebody who wasn't a veteran wouldn't stand a chance because of veterans' preference.

Dunn: It was a standard test at the time of multiple choice questions and answers. To prepare for the test, I went to the public library and picked up the Arco books that were out at that time. Based on what firemen were telling me to do, I sat down in my kitchen on Ferry Street with my future wife at that time. We learned how to go through the Arco book refreshing your mathematics skills, your English diction, basic fire type questions that had been asked around the country. I probably spent three to six months preparing for the examination. My brother didn't do any preparation for the examination. He just felt you could go in and take it. I had left high school early, went into the Marine Corps, and got my GED in the Marine Corps.

I found the test to be very job related. But there was other stuff in the test that if you didn't prepare for it you would have never passed. There are questions that always stay in your mind whenever you take a test. One question was "How long is a fire hose?" How would you ever know how long a fire hose was unless someone in the fire service told you? A fire hose is fifty feet. I'll bet you eighty percent of the guys put down a hundred feet. Today it's all changed, but that's the type of questions.

The written part of the test made up eighty percent of the weight of the examination. If you did well on your written, you did pretty well on the test. The physical was a numbered physical. If you had sit-ups, you had to do a certain number of sit-ups. I don't remember being timed. As long as you could do forty-five sit-ups in a continuous rotation, time wasn't important. Somebody told me, "If you do forty-five push-ups, you'll get a hundred." You just put yourself mentally into a position to do forty-five push-ups. Other people that came on the job with me did extensive workouts. I didn't do that. I just said, "I've got to do forty-five push-ups." and I always practiced forty-five push-ups. I never went to a gym or anything like that. Then the guy says you have to do so many squat thrusts, eighty-two squat thrusts. I did eighty-two. I don't think I could have done eighty-three. I just set myself mentally for that.

I thought the testing was fair and accurate at the time. There were a large number of people taking the test. I think the number of people who took the test was staggering. For someone who was looking for a job, even though we were hiring two or three hundred, there were still two or three thousand people taking the examination at that time. I thought they told you what they expected and I thought the physical part specifically was fair because they told you exactly what they wanted you to do.

Carragher: I took a good written. It had math, ratio and pulleys, a lot of ratio and pulleys, antonyms, synonyms, a couple of questions about fires, I think about extinguishers. Not too deep into fires because they felt they could train you as a fireman when you came on the job. There were questions on county government, the number of counties in the State, the number of legislators in the State, and the type of governor you had. It was all general intelligence. That was the written. Then you had a physical. The physical test at the time consisted of handgrip, sit-ups, pull-ups, chin-ups, a vertical jump, a back lift, kazatskies, the squat jumps. There was also a standing broad jump. I think there were about eight parts. The written counted as six parts and the physical counted as four. That's what they graded you on.

Harris: It was a written exam. I think we had a hundred, a hundred and fifty questions, something like that. I came on with the forty-two hour group, with that exam. I think my standing was two fifteen or something like that and Joe Denardo was two fourteen. After the written, then we did the physical. The physical was way different than what it is today. It was duck squats, the Russian squats, climbing the rope, and running, that's basically what the physical consisted of. You had to pass both and they didn't separate them like they do today, there was no pass/fail. You took the exam and then they called you in to take the second part. Usually within two months you took the other part. I believed they used both scores. They combined them together. What they were doing was establishing a forty-two hour workweek at that time. That's why they took so many men off that list.

Haran: When I came in there was a physical. I took the test when I was twenty-one years old. I wasn't appointed until I was twenty-four and a half. When I was twenty-one years old I was a hundred and fifty five pounds. Back then there was a height requirement. There was a height requirement and a weight requirement. The height might have been five six, five seven. I really don't recall and the weight was somewhere around in the high one forties.

You know this job was in demand. I can remember a lot of fellows were talking about getting themselves stretched the night before the physical or filling up on bananas if they were under weight, trying to make the weight. It was one forty-eight. They might have been one forty-seven. They filled up on bananas and water. But the only bad thing about that is if they made the weight, then they had to take the physical right after that. There were minimums and maximums on the physical. I can remember the course.

I'm forty years on the job and I can remember everything about this fire department prior to coming on. How I studied to get on, working out for the physical, and everything. I took it in the old Sussex Avenue armory, which was on the corner of Jay Street and Sussex Avenue. There was a big armory in there. They tore it down and it's now a nursing facility for elderly. There was a lot of history in that armory. As a matter of fact, they held a rally in there when John F. Kennedy was running for President of the United States.

But getting back to the physical, the first thing we did was push-ups. I believe to get a passing mark in the push-ups you had to do twelve push-ups. To get a mark of a hundred, you had to do fifty-five. I knew that I had to do well because I wasn't a veteran. So, I knew I had to do as many as I possibly could, the maximum of everyone if I could. A disabled veteran or a veteran, they only had to do the minimum because they knew they were going to the top of the list anyhow.

I was in good shape then. I got a hundred in the push-ups. I got a hundred in the sit-ups. Then the next course you went to was a broad jump. You had to jump a certain distance. There was a certain minimum and a certain maximum. I didn't make the maximum, but I almost made the maximum. So, I got a high mark there. Then they had a high jump. You put a piece of chalk in your hand. The monitor would make you stretch out up against a blackboard. You'd mark the blackboard, then you'd squat and you'd jump as high as you could. The mark you made up there, they measured the distance. There was a maximum there and a minimum there. I didn't make the maximum there either, but I got a high mark, close to it.

Then they had a rope climb. You had to climb up. They had a large diameter rope hanging from the rafters in that armory. They had a mark up at eighteen feet. You had to go up hand over hand without the use of your feet. A lot of fellows couldn't even do that. I was able to scramble up that and I got a hundred in that one. Then they had a course that you had to run. What it was from one side of the armory to the other side of the armory. Maybe it was a hundred yards. You took a hockey puck and ran the hockey puck over the other side of the armory. You dropped that hockey puck. You pick another one. You run back. You drop that. You run back again. The whole thing might have been two hundred yards and they timed you in doing that. I believe I got a hundred in that. I was under the time.

The last thing they gave you to do was an exercise called Russian kazatskies. You put your hands behind your head and jumped up and down, alternating bending down on each leg. I don't remember what the minimum number was in that to get a passing mark, but I remember the maximum was eighty-two. You had to do eighty-two of them to get a hundred. I got a hundred. After this you went down the stairs to the locker rooms. Well, everybody's legs were weak because you went from one station to the other doing the physical. There wasn't much time in between, a couple of minutes. That was it.

There were four thousand men who took that test. Everybody wanted that job. They were going from fifty-six hours a week to forty-two. I don't recall how many passed, but I'm sure a lot of men passed. There were a lot of guys taking that physical. You had to do well otherwise you'd be outside looking in. They pushed you through rapidly. So, there wasn't too much time between each exercise. After those Russian kazatskies, everybody was falling down the stairs because their legs were like rubber. I was one of them. I thought I was in good shape, but I had to push everything to the max to do as well as I did. Anyhow I was lucky. I was one of the last five guys appointed to the job off that list, so everything had to go to the max. The little extra that I did in studying for the entrance exam and the extra that I did working out for the physical were the things that made me pass and get appointed to the job. It was an experience to say the least.

Butler: Took the old style civil service test where you had a written, a full physical performance test of sit-ups, squat jumps, vertical leap, a run, push-ups, and then your score for your written was combined with your score for your physical performance test and you were placed on the list.

Written counted for half and your physical counted for a half. I actually finished, in marks, third on the list and was pushed back. When I came on there were a lot of disabled vets around. I wound up forty-first on my list, but actually third in the total marks.

Cody: The test I took was a written test, which they scored in combination with a physical endurance test. Not like what they have now, the agility test. You were scored on how many push-ups you could do; how many sit-ups you could do; how many squat jumps you could do. I remember taking that. I think we all did it until we threw up. So, it was a competitive test. I'm not saying it was the best test in the world. It was a combination of your written mark and your physical mark. If you had the endurance, you could do well.

Garrity: At that time, the test was a standard written intelligence test and a physical. The physical was push-ups, sit-ups, pull-ups, a run, a high jump, squat jumps. I don't remember all of them, but that's the basic test.

McGovern: You took the written one day and the physical another day. You had to pass the written; then you took the physical. That was the old physical with the calisthenics, push-ups and sit-ups. The written was standard, basic knowledge, multiple-choice. I had vet's status, so I placed fourteenth. That was the test that Joe Ricca topped. He came out first on the list. He was in shape. I wasn't. The rest is history.

J. Cosby: It was a multiple-choice written. I really can't remember exactly what the questions were, but it was a lot different from the test today. It was basically you had to pass a written test and you had to pass the physical performance test. You had to pass a background check. When I first came on it was a lot stricter than it is today. They would knock you down for a lot of minor stuff or what would be minor stuff today. It seemed like it didn't necessarily have to be a crime. If they felt like you weren't of good character, they would knock you down. The physical entailed push-ups. You had to do so many push-ups and so many chin-ups. You had to pull a dummy so far. It was as strenuous as the physical you take today. The test now is based on more physical than mental. There was more weight on the written than the physical then.

McDonnell: I took both the police and fire test the same day, the same time. They gave you a fireman's test booklet and a policeman's test. Most of the test was the same. There was just a booklet for each. They pretty much gave you an IQ test. Then there was a fire department test and police department test. It was at Barringer High School. We took the written test and went outside. They let you know if you passed or failed. They called your name. You came up. If you passed you went back inside. You took a medical. There was a doctor. They weighed you. They checked your height. There was a height and weight requirement. They checked your eyesight. You had to have 20/20 vision, couldn't wear glasses. After they did a little basic medical exam on you, then you went and took the physical exam.

The physical exam was basically calisthenics. You had to do pull-ups, push-ups, sit-ups, a squat jump, a shuttle run, and a broad jump. There was a passing mark, that was a seventy and if you did the maximum number you could get a hundred in that particular event. The passing was fairly low. I don't remember. Say you had to do four pull-ups; that was a seventy. A hundred was twelve. I remember the sit-ups were thirty to pass. I got a hundred. There was a number that you did for each event. The passing wasn't really hard. The seventy mark was maybe a third of what a hundred was.

I took the test in September and I didn't get notified until May. I was investigated. In those days they investigated the whole list. There were twenty-six guys in my group. They took the whole list. It was a list of thirty, counting the other four guys. They couldn't get guys. That list came on in June. That same year there was a list in October; there was a list in November; and a list in December. They couldn't get people to come on the job in those days. It wasn't really a popular job. It wasn't like it is now where you get hundreds, thousands of people taking the test.

I don't think the salary was as attractive as it is today. I don't really know what it was. It could have been the population was in flux in the city. Blacks didn't really want to be on the fire department. They were more attracted to the police department. That had something to do with it. People at the time didn't think of getting a job with the city. They didn't think it would be a permanent kind of job. The way the city was in flux and was changing. A lot of people didn't think there was much of a future going into a job with the city.

T. Grehl: We took the police and fire. It was a combined test. The written was a general knowledge test. We took that in the morning. You hung around for about an hour or an hour and a half while they corrected it and if you passed that then you took the physical test, which consists of push-ups, chin-ups, pull-ups, sit-ups, and that was it. The only requirements were police you had to be over five seven and five six was the firemen. I don't know if there was a weight requirement. I really don't know. I assume there had to be. I was like five six and a half and about a hundred and thirty pounds.

The height requirement was the only difference between the police and fire tests. In other words, you could take both. It was a combined test. You could go on either list. But it was just a general knowledge. Nothing specific like it is today on ladders; it was a very basic knowledge test.

Ryan: It was a half written test and a half physical performance test. It was the first test that was more job related as opposed to straight calisthenics. It involved climbing ladders, dragging hose, running up stairs with hose, spatial relations, and of course the standard medical test that you had to go through.

H. Carter: The written wasn't hard. The one difficult question that I remember, "You and your five friends take a taxi ride. The cost of the taxi ride is fifty cents. Each of your friends tips a dime. How much did the taxi cab driver receive from you and your friends?" Difficult math like that.

The only thing that almost killed me was the nuts and bolts. That's when, to show manual dexterity, you had to put the right color and right size bolt on the right stud that was built into the board. When I had taken the test for Irvington a month before Newark, I couldn't get my hands to work. So I practiced and practiced. My father thought I was nuts. I was just bolting and unbolting bolts in the backyard. The first thing I did in Newark was separate them by color and then separate them by this and separate them by that and then put them on. Just as I spun the last one the guy goes, "Time." Just made it.

Then they had this spatial relations thing and I screwed up by thinking that the little pin that held it to the board was a dot that you used to judge spatial relations. You needed five out of ten to pass. I had five. I didn't start to pick up until we went outside to the physical performance and you had to actually climb an aerial. Well, I had been a fireman for a long time, so I just went up the aerial to the roof. Then you had to drag a hose. Being a large chap, I had no problem. I knew that you rolled your shoulder into it and you tugged like a son of a bitch. I had one of the fastest times of the day amongst anybody simply by knowing how to move hose. I passed.

I almost didn't pass the eye station. I wear glasses. The guy said, "You don't have twenty-twenty eye sight." I said, "Wait a minute. I'm wearing glasses, shouldn't that be twenty-twenty?" "Oh, no the machine says." "Listen, this is too important. Let me try the other machine." "Well, I don't know." "Well, I got a lawyer who says. . . ." "Well no, no. Try the other machine." I sat over the machine and it showed me I was twenty-fifteen. But if I hadn't been a loud mouth, I'd have never been a Newark fireman.

Langenbach: The written was a multiple choice test, followed by a physical performance, and then a physical. The written was all multiple choice. I don't think there was true false. That was 1972. I took the physical performance in East Orange at the East Orange firehouse. But I can't remember where I took the written test. I don't think it was Barringer. I thought it was maybe Clifford Scott, but I'm not sure about that.

Luxton: You did a written test which was a multiple choice. I always called it an idiot test. You know, one and one is two, two and two is four, a little bit of math, a little bit of English, a little bit of common sense. You passed that. It was a pass or fail. That entitles you to move on to the next step and the next step was a physical performance test. That's before they had the hose drag and all that. It was an agility run. There were some sit-ups and some pull-ups and some jumping jacks and things like that.

The advantage that you had at that point, you knew how you did in that test. For your size and weight, you had to do twenty-five pull-ups. Well, if you did twenty-five you knew you got a one hundred. You had to do a shuttle run in x number of seconds and if you did it in that time you knew had a one hundred. So anybody in half way decent shape was able to come up with a one hundred. You knew that your minimum score on the written test was a seventy because you passed and you got a hundred here, so I know I got at least an eighty-five. That gave you that advantage.

Of course, veterans went to the top of the list and disabled veterans went to the top of that list. You had the people who weren't veterans, the people who were, and the people who were disabled vets. The disabled vets went first and so forth.

Connell: We had a written test and we were, I believe, the first ones to use firemen based physical testing, dragging hose, running up three flights of stairs carrying a length of inch and a half, pulling a two and a half inch hose line up on a pulley to the third floor. Then there was an agility test, putting screws and nuts together and pegs in round holes and stuff like that. Both the written and the physical counted toward your score.

Pignato: It was a civil service test where they measured your IQ. There's a test booklet that you study. Arco I think was the name of the company that sold the books. They prep you for the test. Used to tell you what was going to be on the test. Myself and three others from Long Branch drove the 50 miles one way to come to the Boy's Club up here to take the classes. At the time it was a statewide exam and you could live out of the city. As long as you lived in the State of New Jersey, you could take the test. So I did.

I scored well enough because I studied my buns off. That was the written part. The practical test was at the East Orange fire department training academy. We had to climb aerial ladders, which I had never done before. I was always afraid of heights. You couldn't get me on a stepladder before I came on this job unless you had a gun up my back, maybe I'd climb up then. The test was to climb an aerial ladder, you had to pull a hose, a two and a half inch hose, over itself and drag it so many feet for time, and then there was a spatial relations part showing your mechanical ability on three dimensional objects. Lining them all up and how they're supposed to look. Not just on paper, but the blocks are actually there and you actually had to do it hands on. There were a lot of hands on things you had to do which showed you mechanical ability. You got graded on that, which is missing today on the fire department. The fellows coming on the job aren't mechanically inclined and this is a mechanical job.

Perdon: At that time they were just starting to make the transition with the type of test. I actually had probably the easiest test that was ever given as far as an entrance. I mean they had the written. This was when they started going away from the push-ups and all that. I probably had one of the easiest physicals going. We had to do a manual dexterity test. We had to play with little screws. Our test probably had the most fire department related stuff. We had to push around, pull around a dummy. We had the hose. Just run with some two and a half and then we had to go up the interior stairs of the East Orange training tower with a hose and then descend by way of the aerial ladder, done deal. That was the physical, probably the easiest one that was ever given. I think it got harder after that.

Langevin: It was a statewide civil service written exam and then a performance physical. I took the written test in Ridgewood High School and the physical at East Orange Training Center in East Orange. The physical consisted of a number of dexterity tests, colorblindness, and then job related skills, hauling hose and running up fire escapes.

The written at that time the written counted toward your final score. After the written test came out, you were notified that you passed or failed and then you were given the date for the physical part. If you passed you were given your rank on the list.

Bisogna: When I took the test, it was basically a five part physical which consisted of hose couplings, climbing an aerial to the fourth story of the training tower in East Orange, matching sugar cubes. This is part of the physical. They had like ten different arrangements of sugar cubes and you had to find the group with the ten different configurations. Then you had to drag a hundred and fifty feet of dry inch and a half hose on the ground, run a course, and run up four flights of stairs. They timed you. That was the physical.

There was a multiple choice written test. I don't remember how many questions, but it was purely multiple choice. It had to do with whether you picked the right tool for tightening a bolt. They had a picture of a screwdriver or a wrench. They had a lot of reading comprehension, math questions. It was a basic multiple choice test for IQ, the kind that they've banned since.

Ricca: The written was a multiple choice. It was the advent of the new physical. I took the physical in East Orange and it was very awkward. They weren't set the way they wanted to do things. They had an aerial ladder a hundred feet in the air that you had to climb and then climb back down. Then they realized that wasn't the way to do it. So they put it to the tower. Hoisting the hose, running inch and half up through the training facility, it was timed. Nuts and bolts, putting the right nut on the right bolt on a piece of wood which came pretty easy for me because I was a mechanic. This is before the shuttle run. It was probably on the titer totter of the shuttle run. It was the first job related type of physical, but it was not job related at all basically. Except for running with an inch and a half hose, you have to have a parameter, but who runs full speed up the stairs with equipment on and inch and a half? It's more important that you get there. Then hoisting the hose, it was funny, there was one kid, he jumped up on the rope, he was so thin with the hose, it out counter balanced him and he just hung there. That was the first agility type, if I might call it, physical from the old push-up, sit-ups, and squat thrusts that were in the past.

Gesualdo: At the time, I guess it would have been around 1977, it was a written test, which was multiple choice, kind of general knowledge, a little back ground in mechanical ability. There was some math on there and then some English. That was followed with a physical. I remember sit-ups, push-ups and a kind of obstacle course situation. Not what they have today, not as elaborate as they have today. That's what I can remember. That was it. I was taking so many tests at the time. I seem to remember them all as being basically the same.

Chapter Four: The Academy

Vetrini: Well, as temporary, they had us up there for about a month. They used our group as a trial set up for the Academy, knowing that they were going to be getting a group of men on. So, they kept us up there a few extra weeks; more or less putting together the training programs they were going to use for the large number of men coming on the job. They were doing a lot of these trials as to how they were going to conduct it. Then when I came on as a regular after a year and a half as a temporary, I still had to go up to the training with the rest of the recruits who were put on from the civil service list.

There were ninety-seven of us put on at the one time from that list. We all went up to the training school. They broke us up in classes by our shift, but at that time we only had two platoons. That was what they called them. When we were off duty during the day we had to go to school, no overtime.

Redden: They couldn't afford to send anybody to the Academy. They had so many holes in the companies. When I went to Two Engine, three of us were assigned; three brand new firemen were assigned to Two Engine. That's how bad the manpower situation was.

Kinnear: I never went through the Academy. They put us on the job. They needed men because it was right after World War II. They were so shorthanded. So they put us right in the firehouse. They put me in Six Engine and the guys were all good to me. They assigned me to one man, a fellow named Johnny Mig. I stayed with Johnny all the time. Borrowed a helmet from somebody; borrowed a rubber coat, and I had bought a pair of boots because my father said buy a pair of boots. I just hopped on the back step and went with Johnny Mig. When he was off, there was another guy they assigned me to. "Do what I do or stay with me. Hold my hand. Oh, eventually we're going to train you." They never got around to it. My formal training was zero, really. I think that went for that whole group and they put on around ninety men.

Masters: We had Chief McCormack as instructor, up on Eighteenth Avenue. They taught us everything pertaining to firematics and hydraulics, about the dress uniform, everything like that. We threw ladders. They had the old Ahrens Fox engines up there, so we learned about hooking up, working the pumps, all of that. We didn't jump into the net. They did away with the net when I was there. Guys used to jump out of the second floor. We didn't do that.

F. Grehl: We went to the Academy for about three weeks in which they gave us the basic fundamentals. The problem being that they needed man power. The 1947, '48, and '49 lists were all depleted almost as soon as they came out. They just had to keep having exams year after year for the three years just to fill the vacancies. So they really couldn't spend time, sending us for a long time at the Academy. There were times other than that, in the 1959 list when they put the forty-two hour work force to work. They put on over a hundred men. They couldn't send these fellows to the Academy because they needed them to fill the spots. That was a real experience when you get a hundred and forty people all of the sudden with no experience and no training at all. Today there are State laws, which make it mandatory that they have a certain amount of hours of training before they are permitted to go into the field.

Vesey: When we first came on we were at the Academy up on Eighteenth Avenue for two weeks. They showed you ladders and basic stuff. They showed you and that was it. After that it was on the job training.

Masterson: I didn't go to the Academy. I went to City Hall. They gave me an envelope, go to Ten Engine. Do you know where it's at? If you don't know, ask this guy. He'll explain it to you. I went over to Ten Engine. Captain Meeker was working. He took me up stairs to his office. He wrote it down that I was assigned. He told me, "You're on Captain Brenner's tour. You'll come in such and such a time to work." I went down stairs and he showed me around a little bit and I went home. I came in with an old turn out coat my father was going to throw out and borrowed a helmet and a pair of boots. Like everybody else in those days, you didn't have anything. You came in, they'd loan you everything. You had to get your helmet at Cairn's, the leather helmet. You had to get it measured. Then it was time to get the boots. You'd find out what turn out coat you needed. With an engine company it's one coat and with a truck it's another coat. Where ever you're working, the coats do make a difference.

Deutch: There were twelve of us who came off the beginning of this new list in '53. And we were put right in the firehouses because of shortages. We had no training. I had no training at all. They said we would eventually get some, but we didn't.

Wall: I went to the Academy on Eighteenth Avenue. Of course, it was a much more abbreviated training than they received when I was training boss. There was no rappelling. They didn't let you do anything that was dangerous. That was the philosophy. I'm serious. And when you questioned the old timers at the time, it was, "Well, in 1920 some guy got killed rappelling, so we don't do it anymore." At that time they were very cautious. Our first introduction to masks was in the basement of the building on Eighteenth Avenue where they set off a couple of smoke bombs. You went down and groped around and came back. They said, "Okay, now you know how to use a mask. Go forth my boy."

Freeman: Yes, we went through on Eighteenth Avenue. That's where we took our training. We went through the hydrants, the wrenches, and the hose. The one thing they didn't do was rappel out the window on the rope. Because previous to our class or somewhere along in there some guy fell out of a window, off the rope. They mentioned that to us. So we didn't do that. We did ladders. We raised ladders. They were wooden ladders then and we climbed ladders. I guess we had instruction on masks. That was it. It wasn't much. I don't even remember how long we went through class. There were twenty-five of us in that class.

McGee: We went to the Academy for maybe ten days. My first day in the firehouse I believe was Christmas Eve. What they taught was all foreign to us, at least to me. I had no previous knowledge and didn't know any firemen. Basically it gave us a rough idea of what the job was in terms of hose and equipment and tools and things like that. They said at the Academy that we would get most of our training on the job in the assignments that we went to.

McGrory: When I did get appointed, we went up to the Academy. The Academy was where headquarters is now. It was only a two-week stint.

What you did was not that involved. You learned the knots and you learned what a line was, what the hose was, and ladders. You climbed ladders. You did different things, but it was pretty basic. They took us down to the dock. Showed us how a pumper would draft, threw an aerial up against the building and stuff like that.

Denvir: We came right to the firehouse and then went to the Academy. There were big groups going through, so a whole tour would go for the two weeks. We had to work.

Smith: We were assigned. When I came on I was assigned to Engine Twenty-one. That was strictly for personnel reasons. We had to attend the Academy on our days off and when we worked nights. I worked days in the firehouse. I worked nights in the firehouse. The time I worked nights in the firehouse, those days I had to go to the Academy. When I was off on a seventy-two, if it was during the week, I had to go to the Academy. If you were normally off on the weekend, then you got off. If you worked weekends, then you worked straight through. You never got any time off.

Charpentier: We went to the Academy about a month after we were on the job. Our initial training was with the older men of the company. My captain went through all the equipment and how to use it, what to do, what not to do. Don't forget a whole complete tour went on, which they split up among all four tours. They couldn't send everybody because they wanted to start the fourth tour. So, about a month or so after, we went to the Training Academy for a couple of weeks. We didn't go full time. When we worked nights and our days off, we were in the Academy. When we worked nights, we were in the Academy from eight o'clock in the morning to maybe three or three thirty. Then we had to go report to our company for six o'clock.

Dunn: Our training academy at that time was up on Eighteenth Avenue. Honestly, we did a lot of drilling out of the books, a lot of talking, but we didn't do any field experience. What we had to do was work our regular field assignment at night. So we were in the firehouse while we were going to the Academy. The training was geared strictly to book learning, regular classroom type of instructions. We used the Oklahoma's and a lot of old notes that the captains had accumulated over the years. There was no real standard for what we were going to do. Then when we got done with the Academy, we went right back to the firehouse, which today, union-wise, you wouldn't do. We were actually working very strenuous hours. In fact, if they had a bad night the guys in the busy companies would show up in the morning half dead. Then sit in the classroom, so by ten o'clock they would all probably be sleeping. The lights would be out, the movie would be on, and they would sleep through half the day. So the training lacked. What we lacked in the training we were picking up because we were already in the firehouses. Every firehouse had new members assigned to it, so you weren't like an outcast. It would be two or three people assigned to the company who were new members at that time.

The Newark Fire Academy then wouldn't even relate to the Academy as we know it today. It just wasn't designed that way. The people assigned there were elderly, ready for retirement. They were in the twilight of their career. The captains in there were more military and very stand-offish, probably based on being in a World War I type of military. The average student was probably twenty-one to twenty-five and our instructors were between fifty-eight and sixty-five. Most of them had been out of the field for some time. They had been in the Academy for quite some time. They had a little trouble with the younger people coming with younger ideas asking them why are we doing something or "Why are we doing this. I've been in the firehouse for a month and we haven't done this yet? Why are we talking about this type of thing?" So it was almost an adversarial type of contest between the instructors, who would be the military dictator, and the young and aggressive people coming in off the city streets after World War II with a much more liberal attitude. I thought the people at the Academy had a much harder time understanding the younger people, our values, and the way we were thinking.

I guess it probably exists today, too. You become very complacent in your job after so many years. You realize you're not going to change it. You see the young firemen running around the Academy. You say "What the hell are they running like that for? They're not going to run like that. We're not going to do that." But again that's just your seniority showing itself. The Academy at that time lacked a lot but it was made up for by the large number of new young captains in the fire department because of the change of hours. Everyone was studying because they didn't know how to be captains and we didn't know how to be firemen. So it became a working arrangement really for both of us to learn from each other.

Carragher: I went to the Training Academy up on Eighteenth Avenue where headquarters is today for four weeks. It was strictly full time days. Deputy Chief Schoettly was head of the Academy. He retired somewhere in the late '60s. Captain Murray was up at the Training Academy and Captain Meeker. It was a nice course. There were a total of seventeen in my class. We learned the fundamentals, hose layouts, hose stretches, hose couplings, ladder parts, ladder raises, knots, and how to tie knots. What the knots are used for. Basic hydraulics, they taught us first aid. We had a thirty-hour first aid course while we were there. Joe O'Conner was a first aid instructor up there at the time.

They taught the use of hand tools, axes; the use of hydrants. Basically everything we'd need. Some mask training, at the time the Burrell mask was the big one. But they did show us the Chemox and the Scott air pack. I don't know if they've changed too much. We did a lot of ladder evolutions, hose evolutions. Never had a fire, they didn't light fires at the time; jumped out the second floor window into the life net. Then you had a vertical raise where you raised a twenty-eight foot ladder vertically. You had to go up one side of the ladder, climb over the top, and come down the other. They raised ground ladders, three-man raise on a thirty-five and then they did a five or six man raise on a forty-five with the Bangor poles. I don't think they showed us anything on the pumps at the time. No driving, no pumping, it was strictly what they could teach at the Academy.

Haran: I didn't go to the Academy before the firehouse. I went down to City Hall on a Monday morning and got sworn in. There were five of us who were sworn in. They said they had all our assignments and I was going to Salvage One on the fourth tour. I was the only guy who didn't go to a truck company or an engine company. I went to Salvage One. They said, "We're not sending you guys to the Academy because we're having a class coming up pretty soon. When we have more fellows coming on, we're going to send you guys to the Academy." Nine months later, they put about eight or nine fellows on. But that was off another list. They had run another test and they had another list. There were about fourteen or fifteen of us nine or ten months later who went to the Academy. Actually we didn't have an Academy back then. It was more or less just classrooms set up on

Eighteenth Avenue where fire headquarters is today. They had classes on the first floor. There was partial training like stretching hose, but there was no fire tower there or anything like that. You just went in and attended classes. After being eleven months on the job and being in Salvage, they sent us for twelve weeks. We went there for twelve weeks, five days a week from eight to four o'clock.

When you go to the Academy, they give you basic training. You don't get into advanced things. You're not going to get into formulas or pumping or anything like that. You learn all that when you get out into the firehouse. They give you the basics. After being on for eleven months, going up there for twelve weeks got quite boring. There were other fellows there who had just come on.

Just a little story, while we're in the Academy. There was a fellow who lived in my neighborhood by the name of Jimmy Elwood. He came on about nine months after me. I started the Academy with him. I grew up with Jimmy. He was sort of a character on this job, very smart, funny, witty guy. He was a laugh a minute. I had a car at that particular time and we were driving up Eighteenth Avenue going to the Academy. He lived a couple of blocks from me, so I used to pick him up in the morning and took him up there to the Academy. I had my gear in the trunk. My gear was eleven months old, but his gear was brand new. Never the less, you want to protect your gear. Not only because it protects you, but the fact that it's expensive. We came out of the Academy to go home at four o'clock and my car was gone. Somebody stole my car while I was at the Academy. Here's all our gear in the trunk. Now, when we were at the Academy, we were going to respond to multiple alarm fires. That was the deal. If you're in the Academy training and a multiple alarm fire came in the City, a second alarm or better, you were going to respond to it. Well, we had no gear. Now, he's cursing me. Telling me, "God, I just spent all this money for the gear and now I don't have it. You better call your insurance company." But, eleven days later they found my car parked down in back of the old city hospital. The front end was all pushed in. It was damaged, but thank God our stuff was still in the trunk of the car. So, we got it back eleven days later.

Butler: At the time I went right to the firehouse, to Truck Eleven, tour two. I replaced a firefighter by the name of Bobby Regan who was assigned to the Arson Squad when I was appointed to the fire department. I had approximately four months in the company while there was additional hiring. In the first or second week of May the heads of department decided to hold a training academy class up on Eighteenth Avenue, which is now Fire Headquarters building.

I learned very little in the Academy then because I had four months of training out in the field already. I was with an excellent group of firefighters. I was in the truck and at that time the roll call of the truck was an officer and five men, with the engine having an officer and four men. A lot of young but experienced, four, five year experienced firefighters who took me right with them, took me right under their wing and gave me some very good valuable lessons on how the real world was out there and not how the book teaches you to do it. The only thing I learned maybe in the Academy might have been possibly a little more of the rules of the fire department because I didn't have much of that. How things were supposed to work in the fire department and the actual rules and regulations and what General Orders were all about. But as far as actual firefighting techniques, I learned very little in the Training Academy.

Highsmith: They sent us to the Academy December the 16th, 1963. We stayed in the Academy for one week and then my first assignment was Engine Company Nineteen, Fenwick and Frelinghuysen Avenue. I went back to the Academy for thirty days in May. Fourteen of us came on together. They really didn't have enough for a full Academy and being in December vacations start coming up, they put the new recruits out there in the field. We had thirty guys. Boisy Cosby was the only other black. He had been on the job for two or three years, so there was nothing that they could teach him. He was from Five Truck on Belmont Avenue, a fast house. Nothing they could teach him.

On our graduation day, they burnt down a house for us on Rose Terrace, a vacant house. They doused it with gasoline. When they lit that house up, it turned into a two alarm fire for real. People started coming down. The bells started hitting. Engines started coming. Actually, the recruits weren't alarmed. We had fully charged lines and all knew we had to back out and put water on it, but all of the veterans were afraid for us. We put the fire out. It just got out of hand, but was a lot of fun. They even wrote it up in the paper. Fire burnt for recruits gets out of hand, turns into a two alarm fire. It was a big joke to us. We had a nice little party after we got finished. All those guys who I went to the Academy with, I still see them. I talk to them. Still have that same feeling that we had then, because we were all young kids. I was twenty-one years old.

Cody: I went right into the field. Actually I went to the Academy for four days. We were appointed on a Monday and we went Tuesday through Friday. Then we went right into the field. We worked about a year. When they had enough for a class then everyone went back.

Garrity: I had three days training before I went into the firehouse. We did a little mask work on the Burrell filter masks. We did some ladder climbing and squirted some water with a hose and that was it.

McGovern: I was on three years before they put me through a two-week course. You got appointed on we'll say a Monday then Tuesday I had to report to the firehouse. That's the way it worked.

Prachar: I was in the field two years before I went to the Academy. It was very difficult because you learn out in the field. You do in the Academy what you have to do, but you learn on the job. Why did we have to go back to the Academy and learn how to put a mask on? Learn the proper way of pulling ceilings, how to open windows. In the basement of Special Service, they had pumps. Went over there, worked the pumps. It was a joke is what it came down to, but it was for insurance purposes. They had to do this. We had the life nets back then; had to learn how to properly use the life net. Jump out the second floor window into the life net. The Academy at the time was up on Eighteenth Avenue where headquarters is now. It was just basic and it was a two-week course. It was probably the most boring two weeks I ever put in on this job.

There were guys who were on before me. They were on three, three and a half years maybe. They were in my class. Back at that time, they just wanted to get you into the field. If you didn't know anything, you had a little bit of a problem because it was scary. I rode with Rescue and I rode with Ten Engine as a buff before I came on the job. I was lucky to work with a couple of captains in those houses where they would let me stay with them. Let me go in. Not when the fire was going full bore, but when the fire was knocked down. Let me use the line. With Captain Juliano from Rescue, I always carried a hook. He would take me in later on, open up a window, how to properly search. I was taught by him when I was a buff. Going through rooms; turning over the mattress, this way somebody knows you were there.

So I was fortunate enough that I learned before I came on. Where the other guy I came on with, John Missiggia, he had no idea. I came on with another guy, Bill Waters. He had no idea what was going on. In fact, Bill Waters was assigned to Four Engine. On his first run out the door, he didn't realize he had to hold onto the bar. When they took off out the door, he was left lying on the apparatus floor. It sounds dumb, but if you don't teach people, they don't know. So, I lucked out there, but to go back after two years it was really a joke.

Pianka: We went straight to the firehouse. A year later I went to the Academy. They taught us more or less the same thing I had been doing for the year prior to that. It was just redoing things. We did a little practical training and a little classroom work. They would take us out and we would pull ceilings in abandoned buildings and we jumped into the rescue net. They didn't have a smoke house at the time. But probably more or less what you do now. That's the big difference now; they have the facilities down there where you have the smoke.

You know what, I don't know if we missed it that much. I came on in May. The rest of the guys who came off that list came on in June. The next list came on in October, November. That's essentially the crew that went down there, so most of us had field experience. It was okay. I don't say we shouldn't have done it, but I don't think any of us would have missed it. The firemen take care of you. If you were with a good crew, the guys took care of you. They taught me everything I needed to know. It was first hand and they would watch over me. And nothing compared to bouncing out that front door on that first day I tillered. In a way it's a tough way to learn, but it stuck with me for the rest of my life because two, three years later, we're going down Clinton Avenue. We hit a bump. The wheel pops out on the tiller and now I have to keep a cool head and get it back in.

McDonnell: When my class went on, we went to the Academy for two days over the Memorial Day weekend and that was unusual. I think we only went for two days because there was the group of us. We all got put on. They gave us a little run down of the Fire Department. The Academy was on Eighteenth Avenue then where Fire Headquarters is now. The only one I remember there was Kossup. He was there. Stienbach might have been there, too. Crowley, I think was in charge of it then. We went for two days in June. We were told we had to go get our uniforms. They had just switched over to the blue uniforms from the khaki pants and the chambray shirts. That was in 1970 sometime. By June we had to wear the blue uniforms. So, we had to go out and buy blue uniforms. We went through two days. They gave us whatever they could teach us in two days. At least they gave us a little orientation.

Rotonda: You went more or less right to the firehouse. You came on. You went to the firehouse. I think about a year after, that's when they started up on Eighteenth Avenue. Some guys were on even longer, maybe a year more than me. Then we went to the Academy up on Eighteenth Avenue at that time for a course or whatever it was. But you learned more on the job than you did anything else, on the job training.

T. Grehl: I didn't go straight to the Academy. I walked into the firehouse in red, white, and blue sneakers and white pants. Captain Lardiere was sitting there waiting for me, my first captain. He told me, "Have a cup of coffee kid, relax. I'll show you the firehouse in a minute or two." The bell hit, it was a real good old garbage junk fire with a lot of tires and my white pants became black. I took a lot of heat for that for years. My red, white, and blue sneakers I tried to save. The white pants, I just threw them away. There's no way of saving anything from a tire fire. Needless to say bright white pants didn't make it.

We were brought back to the Academy for training. I'm going to only guess like four, six weeks. When they brought everybody back, a couple people came on before me, seven of us came on together, and I believe approximately eight to ten people came on after us. We did the training up at Eighteen Avenue. So we were limited to what our class could do. Eighteenth Avenue as you know it now, basically where the Arson Squad is and where the chief's office is, that was a bay and that was your classroom. For years that was our Training Academy.

We only did book knowledge because it was a little bogus for them to teach us to stretch hose. We'd been doing it for a month or two months already in the field. But I guess there were certain criteria you had to go through in a training class. The instructors at the time were Director Kossup, I believe he was a Battalion Chief, Chief Wall, and I believe it might have been Chief Morgan. Just recently I reminded Director Kossup that he had promised whoever came out first in the Academy was going to get two days off. This is prior to personal days, before contracts. So I was lucky enough to come out first, but after that he told me "You can't have the days. The Chief told me, 'You can't have the days because there's no contract.' I can't just give you days off." I reminded Director Kossup that he still owes me two days from 1971. So he told me I can have three now.

Ryan: I was in the first class of the new Academy and we spent a month down there. We learned everything from basic terminology used in the fire service to learning evolutions with hose, ladders, Bangor ladders, driving apparatus, basically the whole gamut up to pumping. It was pretty comprehensive for the time, and then of course self-contained breathing apparatus. We didn't have a live burn in the tower. The tower was brand new. There was no paving down here. As I said, it was the first class.

H. Carter: We were the first twelve guys to graduate out of the recruit school. If you know the Academy in 1991 with its paved parking lots and everything, we were here when the fire tower had just been built; the smokehouse had just been renovated; and the entire area was a rubble strewn lot. It was a pain in the butt raising ladders.

I almost got killed. We were out there raising ladders. We used to do the church raise to test people's confidence, where you had the thirty-five foot ladder fully extended straight up with ropes in four directions for steadiness. I'm climbing up the ladder. I just about get to the point where you go up and over to come down the other side and one of the nitwits on the rope slacks up and I start wobbling on the top of the ladder back and forth, back and forth. Eddie Wall, who's now at the US Fire Administration, comes out. He yells at the top of his lungs, "Get that man off the top of that ladder before he falls off the ladder and kills four or five guys." To this day Eddie Wall remembers that story, like eighteen years later. But we graduated.

Langenbach: We went to the Academy before you were assigned to the firehouse. For six weeks I think it was. There were twelve of us who came through the first class. We were in the first class to come through this academy. They were still building the tower. The parking lot wasn't paved. It was still stone. For a lot of the practical stuff, we went to firehouses. We went to Rescue to learn how to jump into the net when Rescue was on Mount Prospect. We went to Seven Engine and did something with Seven Engine. We went to Five Truck and worked with them on the saw and ladders and stuff like that. All of the classroom stuff was done here and some practical things were done here, but most of it was done out on the street.

We were throwing ladders on the gravel. In fact this is where we almost lost Harry Carter. Chief Wall was the boss down here then. We did the church raise. You had to climb a fully extended ladder to get to the top. Then you had to put a ladder lock in and lean back. Well, Harry was as big then as he is now, maybe bigger. When he got up there we almost lost him in the Passaic River. I think that's the way he was leaning.

Luxton: We were the first class in the new Fire Academy when it was fully functional. Eddy Wall was down there. Stanley Kossup, I guess, had just been promoted to Deputy. Bobby Miller had just been promoted to Battalion Chief and Jimmy Nolan was there, Captain Wegans and Stienbach. Carl Duerr, I think, was still a fireman. So, I went through that. I think we were there for six or eight weeks. I had had a little bit of training at a fire school in Mahwah. Nutley didn't give you much. They sent you to fire school up there.

In Newark there were written exams and a lot of lectures. People like Miller and Jimmy Nolan. They brought other people in. Otis elevator came in. There were a lot of different things. Then there was some practical; hose stretching and ladder evolutions and things like. I think a lot of it was as it is today because the facility on Jersey Street was brand new. We were the first ones to have a fire in the smoke house and the first ones to use the training tower as a training tower. I think we did rappelling. Barney Baldino was the Captain at Rescue on the second tour. I remember him coming down with Owen Donnelly and rappelling off the building, showing us how to do that and the slide for life.

You were straight Academy. I don't even remember being loaded into vans and going off to a fire. I don't know whether we had vans at the Training Academy at the time. We had a good class. Out of that class, ten of us are officers, so it was a good class.

Perdon: We were in the Academy for about a month. Basically they taught pretty much the same stuff they teach now. You had your different type teachers there. Chief Ryan was there. He was from the Third Battalion, but he was very knowledgeable in hydraulics and stuff and tried teaching it that way. Forget about it. It was everybody was like, "Yeah, right," with the formulas and everything. We had to come in on Saturdays, a couple of Saturdays, and do some drills, basically all about the same stuff. We had the live burns. I remember doing the church climb with the ladder. I was with Donny Gilmartin and Harry Halpin. So, they're all big boys. I remember they're looking at me and when I came on I was one forty-five wet. This is when you had the guys with the rope and you hold it up in the middle of the air. They were saying, "You're not holding us." So, I had to go up first, go up and down, because they couldn't think I could hold them, big old Donny. Donny said, "Nope, you get your ass up there." Harry, Harry was good people. It's a shame, Harry.

Pignato: We were there for six weeks. We did everything. We had three good instructors. They had just promoted a gaggle of chiefs. I don't know why they had promoted so many chiefs, but almost all of our instructors were chiefs down here. We did everything, a lot of ladder raises. We tillered. We drove. We went to classes, had a lot of smoke house training. It was pretty good. It was all the stuff I had before in the volunteers, but it was pretty good.

Almost everybody in my class was a veteran. So as far as being a para-military organization in the academy, it went pretty smooth because we knew how to cheat the system. The Chief was Chief Wall and his first orientation speech in front of our family members was I want to raise the level of firefighter, and the professionalism like the cops. The cops had reciprocity through out the country, where if they leave Newark and they want to be a cop in California, they could just about get hired out there because they're pretty well trained. Firemen don't have that option.

Chief Wall wanted to bring the level of firefighter up by instituting college courses at Jersey City State College and Essex County College. His theory of making the fire department better went down hill, but at that time we all believed it. A lot if us went back to school at night or during the daytime at Jersey City State or Essex County College to better ourselves for the all brand new fire department that was going to be coming in the future.

We were actually the first real class through here. The class before us came off the same list, Chief Carter, Langenbach, and those guys, six or eight of them. The tower was under construction, so they didn't actually have a full-fledged academy. They say they were the first class, but our class was first.

Langevin: Yes, I was part of the second graduating class of the Newark Fire Department Training Academy. We spent six weeks here. At the time Deputy Chief Wall was commandant. We started from the bottom. Learn the basics. They really didn't care whether you had previous firefighting experience or not. They taught you from the bottom up.

Bisogna: We had six weeks in the Academy. We had Chief Morgan down there. Chief Wall was in charge. There were only fourteen of us in the class, so it was pretty low keyed. But they got a lot of training in the six weeks. We had a lot of live burns, a lot of oil fires, Christmas trees, cars fires. They kept us pretty active. No silly marching or anything like that, it was basically fire training and it was good.

They seemed pretty strict in the beginning, but I was young too and impressionable. After they started horsing around, you said, "This can't be too bad." It was fun. I had a good time in the Academy. We had a bunch of characters in my class. I guess every class does. The guys down there were firemen, but they were fun. They were down there because of whatever reason they were down there.

Ricca: I came on in a class of twelve with nine cadets, cadets that were going to drive the ambulance. They later joined into the fire department. From what I understand, every one of those cadets became a fireman except one fellow who left the police department, became a cadet and went back to the police department. I can't even remember his name, but it was a small class.

We had pretty good training. I think back then the job was a little different. The Academy wasn't that old at the time either, in '74. I think it was a little bit more military from what I've seen. But there was time for play. I guess this job is good with humor and there's always somebody doing a practical joke or something like that. The fitness part of it, I thought was a good deal. We had a little bit more physical training.

We had a lot more equipment to train with back then. They would think nothing of bringing down a full assignment. You'd go out there and there'd be four engines, two trucks, everybody but the Chief. There were more companies around too though. I saw the demise of at least a half a dozen companies closed since I've been on the job. But that's probably the only difference I can see.

I believe it was an eight week course. They went over the mask, a lot of time in the smoke house. Stienbach was one of the captains. It was known in the Academy that I could tiller. So, he came back to me, he used to call me Angelo. He said, "Angelo, could you tiller?" I said, "I never tillered before, but I heard my brothers talk about it." So, I actually broke in some of the guys tillering when I had no idea how to do it myself. But Stienbach took us once around the Academy grounds. He says, "You got the feel of it?" I said, "Yeah." Bang, we were right out on McCarter Highway next thing I knew. And he had the guys driving. Everybody had their turn.

We had your basic courses. We did all of that. They worked out of the ventilation book a lot and went over engine company operations. Harvey Wiegan stood up underneath the monitor and said, "If you go to the hot dog wagon and ask for a hot dog, don't flash your badge for that hotdog." Everybody was looking at each other and not realizing what he was saying, but he was more or less telling us don't use any influence because you're a fireman to get anything free. And that was his analogy, the way he put it, but it took like two or three days before somebody said, "Oh, that's what he was talking about." We would look at each other because we had no idea where the heck he was coming for. I think Captain Wiegan was Salvage 2, but I'm not sure. That had been another one of those companies that were disbanded before I came on. As a matter of fact, I think he was always a captain in Salvage 2, his first assignment.

Gesualdo: I went through the Academy in June of '78. I don't remember. Everything's kind of like a blur. They used us pretty quickly for summer vacations, so I would think it was only a matter of maybe initially two weeks, maybe ten days. And then out in the field and then we went back for a while, but it was a very short time. It was definitely worth going through, the few days, but as far as going back, I think at that time in the middle '70s when there was a lot of work, everybody felt kind of, "Well, you can't teach me anything else."

In the Academy, I learned it was a whole lot different than European firefighting. It wasn't as regimented. I was very surprised. In England anyway and from being over there I heard Germany was the same, France. That they have a more structured regimented Academy. We were in the Academy for three months when I went to England. That was five days a week, home only on the weekends if you could afford the train. Because we did our training up in the London area and at the time I was living down near Oxford with my wife and kids. So, you were there five days a week and you had a schedule. Every hour you knew what you were doing.

They did allow for mid-day breaks, physical training breaks, which consisted of like volleyball, tug of war, team sports, rugby, things like that. And then back to work until about five o'clock in the evening. It was para-military much more than here because the British Fire Brigade at that time consisted of ninety percent ex-military people. So, I remember it being a lot more "Yes, sir" "No, sir" kind of like basic training.

Whereas the Newark Fire Academy was a little less structured and a kind of story telling type. There wasn't really the emphasis on some of the things that should have been emphasized like climbing ladders and things like that. In England it was every day, twice a day you did ladder exercise. And you had better be able to run up a ladder by the time you got done. Where in Newark it didn't seem like it was really that important whether you could really go up a ladder efficiently or not. At that time in England they where still using the pompier ladders. We did a little bit of training with that. They had the wheeled escape ladders, a different assortment of ladders. So, when you got out of the Academy, you knew how to climb a ladder. I really don't believe that the emphasis was there in Newark.

But other than that, it was interesting. I had been in the service. I knew pretty much how to act, when to cut up, when not to cut up. Some of the younger guys had a little harder time with that even though in Newark it was a little less structured. If they had gone to the one in England, they would have definitely matured a lot quicker. But it was very informative. The instructors were good. They were kind of a little more down to earth, reachable than the ones in England. They kind of stood off, the officers and ranking personnel in the Fire Brigade there.

Training, they tended to stay back a little bit and not let you get too close, whereas at least with Newark, you were able to get a little personable with people. If you had a problem you didn't feel uncomfortable going to them with it. So that had an advantage down here, the relaxed atmosphere here. But other than that they were both very informative, just one focused more on technique and repetition where in Newark they just gave it to you as quick as they could and got you out into the field because they needed replacements.

Chapter Five: Ethnic Origins

Fredette: When I went to Six Engine, the man whose place I took had 27 years seniority and he was last on his tour for vacation pick. He came on in 1917. Mostly all of his crew came on in April of '17 and he came on around August, September of 1917. So that meant that he was the last one on his shift and they all stayed together. All Germans, spoke it and all. They had German newspapers going to the firehouse.

Redden: The ethnic makeup of the department when I came on was German and Irish. At that time the Italian group was moving up in numbers, but it was just beginning. Years ago it had been a German Department, then it became predominantly Irish, and then the Italians came on. From then on it was quite a mixture. The Italians came on in large numbers with the 1959 list. When Willie Thomas came in, we start getting the blacks.

The discipline on the department came from the German officers. And also from my group that came on right after the war. We were used to discipline. We were used to respecting authority. You didn't question an order. You did what you what you were told. There was discipline. Discipline was rigid. I lived that for three years in the service. Most fellows lived that three, four years in the service, so it was nothing new.

Kinnear: When I came on the department was predominantly Irish, a few Germans, and some Italians. I think the biggest race that gained right away were the Italians. I think more of them started coming into town and changed it to an Irish-Italian job. And of course, the blacks started coming in. I think Willie Thomas came on in the early 50's. He was the first one. I guess there was some resentment. I never worked directly with him. I guess there were some people who didn't like it; who wouldn't accept it. I found that in the beginning anyway, the ones who came in were pretty decent guys.

Masters: Oh, the department was predominantly Irish. When I went to Eleven Engine, Eleven Truck I was the only Italian. We had another Italian who came in later, the next year, Cordesco.

F. Grehl: The department was basically Irish and German when I first went on the job. Then the Italians came, Polish came. More and more Italians to the point where I guess now the fire department is basically Italian. Blacks I guess are taking over, too. But I still think Italians probably are the most prominent ones. So, it was basically Irish and German. The Police Department was basically the same way, Irish and German. It had changed after the war when a lot of the people came home and they all took these civil service jobs. Veterans, hey you're on top of the list and they cleaned all the lists off.

McCormack: Again I guess, I would say at the time I came into it, it was primarily Irish. But I worked with old timers who had a good number of years on the job. Some of them were Irish. Some of them were German. I had some German fellows that I worked with. And most of the younger fellows at the time I came in were Irish.

Masterson: The fire department started out basically German and Irish and Italians just start to move in. I think Tangretti, Morris Tangretti, he worked with me at Ten Engine on the other tour, was one of the first Italian captains. Danny Tauriello was another Italian. It starts to become Italian and Irish. But basically it was German, German and Irish I think. Then the Italians came in and they moved up to it. Then of course the blacks came in.

Wall: Okay, a lot of Irish obviously, Germans, a good number of Italians. When I came on the job there was one black guy, Willie Thomas. Then a black guy came on with me, Shelly Harris. Shelly Harris came on with us. So, in '54 there were two black guys, Willie Thomas and Shelly Harris. We didn't see a lot more black guys until the forty-two hours when I think something like eight or ten black guys were appointed.

McGee: The department was mostly Irish and Italian. By that time the German influence had sort of started to wane. I image prior to me coming on it was probably mostly German and Irish and then it became Irish and Italian and then it became pretty much anybody. Then little by little the black and the Puerto Rican/Spanish element started to come on the job. But when I first came on it was primarily Irish and Italian.

Freda: I think the fire department in the early days from what I've heard and this is pure stories that I've heard from old timers, was kind of wild. Then it changed to being very strict when the predominance of officers was German. We couldn't even say semi military. We're going into military. They ran things with an iron hand, the stereotype German. And then they got that way and stayed that way for a while.

Charpentier: I would say ninety percent Catholic. Don't forget, when I came on, that list had over two hundred men appointed off it. So, I would say it was a mixture. I think there were ten or twelve blacks who came off my list. We had a bunch of good blacks come off that list, too. The likes of

Timmy Henderson, a few others I can't think of right now, a bunch of good firemen. Italians, Irish, Germans, a few other different groups. I think there were one or two Spanish came on out of that list. But it was a mixture. I couldn't say it was fifty percent Irish or fifty percent German or anything. I would say maybe seventy or eighty percent Catholics.

When I came on I would say maybe there were ten blacks. Willie Thomas was the first. Then there were maybe ten who came on prior to my list.

Smith: The men in Ten Engine, I'd been around men of that vent all my life. Basically they were Irish, Irish-German, or Italian or Polish. The majority religion was Roman Catholic. So that didn't differ any from my friends who I grew up with. The only difference was that these men were from World War II. I was from Korea and there really wasn't that much of a gulf between us. Because they were the early part of the Depression and I was the back end of the Depression. We still shared a cultural identity, religion, and the deprivations of the Depression. To talk in a sense you might say, you walked in and you were absorbed. It was homogeneous.

Miller: The department at that time, I'd say was ninety five percent Caucasian. There were very few blacks on the job at the time. Ethnically, German, Irish, and Italian were predominant. Most of the people who I worked with were German, Irish and Italian. Of course, some of the houses were more Italian or more Irish and German than others. But the mixture was well balanced.

Carragher: Ethnically, I would say mostly German, Irish. We had some black firemen then. Willie Thomas was one of the first. Right now

Richie Freeman is still on, Shelly Harris, Reggie Evelyn, Cliff Evelyn. They're the ones I worked with offhand that I knew. '59 we got quite a few more who came on. I came on with John Coxan in Five Truck, who died a couple of years after he came on the job. And Fisher, Elton Fisher was in Seven Truck. He retired a couple of years ago. I don't think the minorities were too many at the time. I would say probably if there were thirty to forty, would probably be high out of eleven hundred and eighty people.

Harris: When I came in the department, I would say, it was mostly Irish. I would say a good sixty, seventy percent Irish and then we had a few blacks. It was a very small number. There weren't that many Germans in the department or if they were German, I didn't know them. Maybe because they worked in the other houses and I didn't get to know these people. But Captain Leber was the only one I knew. Mostly Irish and Italian, that was what I saw in the Fire Department. The Germans may have been here, but I think that as the Irish moved in, then a lot of Germans may have retired or left the job. Even in the Police Department, you had a lot of Germans. Then it became Irish, then to the Italians, and then the blacks started coming in.

Cahill: The job was probably, ninety-nine percent white with pretty good cross section of ethnic groups. A lot of the chief officers were probably still Irish. The Irish majority was certainly disappearing. It was a pretty good cross section when I came in.

Butler: At the time I came on it was predominantly Irish and Germans, with Italians making inroads too. As time went on you started to get a lot more Italian fellows coming on. Italians really started to pop in. The only Irish or Germans that you really had coming forward were sons or nephews or something of the old time firemen. But then as the years went on, of course, you had the minorities come on. You had some blacks at first; then you had a push for not only blacks but Hispanics coming on the job. So, the years went on and the makeup racially changed from an almost lilywhite department to a mixed department.

Garrity: Believe it or not, when I went to Two Truck I was an ethnic minority. The only Irishmen in the place at the time were Tommy Boyle, myself, and Dennis Cogan. It was Irish, Italian, and German. That was throughout the whole fire department. There were some blacks obviously. I don't remember any Hispanics at that time. But that was the basic makeup of the fire department. Predominantly Irish, all the chiefs we had were Irish. At the time there were probably ten or fifteen blacks that I could even think of if I went back that far. Ronnie Heath was one, Phil Jackson, who's up in the Bureau now, Len Minitee. I can't think of too many more, but I know there were more than three. There were a couple in Twelve Engine, a couple in Eleven Engine I think, on Bergen Street there were a couple there, but probably not more than twenty that I can actually think of back then.

Knight: There were Irish firehouses. There was no doubt about it. You could go over to Central Avenue, to Eleven Engine and Eleven Truck. That was primarily Dublin over there. If you weren't Irish nine out of ten times you wouldn't feel comfortable there. The house I was in on Bergen Street, we were a mixed group. We had Germans over there, a couple of Polish, a couple of Irishmen, and a couple of Black guys. When I left Bergen Street in January of '65, I went over to Three Truck over on West Market and Hudson Streets. I put seventeen beautiful years in over there and our house was not primarily an Irish house. We had Italians. We had

Germans. We had Irish. We had Polish. You know, it was just an ethnic mix. We didn't start getting black guys into our house until the early '70's. But still there were a lot of houses in the city of Newark that were primarily all white houses, all Irish houses, all whatever. And it was tough for people to break in.

McGovern: When I came on the job, I'd say it was ninety percent white. There weren't that many minorities for some reason. The Police force was I'd say sixty-forty at the time or maybe sixty-five – thirty-five, but the Fire Department for some reason had very few minorities then. There were a handful of blacks who were on longer then I was; who made a career out of it. But in '68, I'd estimate ninety percent white.

Ethnically, just guessing, I'd say the department was forty percent Irish, maybe twenty, twenty-five percent Italian, the rest a mix. I'm just guessing. There were a lot of Irish guys for some reason.

Prachar: Yes, I would say at the time it was probably about ninety to ninety-five percent white, but blacks just then starting to come on. You had quite a few who were on, who came on with the fifty-nine list. The day I was appointed, I came on with a black guy. There were four of us who were appointed that day. One left the job that day. He decided later in that afternoon that he didn't want to be fireman. He was a Newark cop and he wanted to go back to Newark Police, so he got sworn in and resigned the same day. That left three of us, so one out of three was a minority coming on the job. You could see it as the years were going on, more and more are coming. Now, I'm really not sure what the ratio is. I would say it's probably seventy thirty maybe less, maybe closer to sixty forty. But with everything going on they will surpass the white within the next five six years. Depending on how the tests go.

McDonnell: I think when I came on the job there were probably more Irish people than anything. There were a lot of Italians though. I don't think Irish people were fifty percent of the job. It was still basically Irish and Italian though. I think the German influence was gone. I heard older guys say that was where the discipline came from, the old German officers. They were stern. That's where the discipline in the department came from.

Pianka: There were a lot of Irish and German on the job because historically and traditionally that's what this job was. Out of a thousand men maybe you had less than a hundred, a hundred black guys on the job. But there were a lot of Italians, Irish, German, and some Polish people. I think most of the people on the job, up to my point anyway, grew up in the city.

Langenbach: The job was predominantly white. On Belmont Avenue, there was only one black guy on my tour, on the fourth tour. Dick Freeman was in Twelve Engine. The third tour was, let's see, it was almost all black in the engine. The truck was all white. In the truck, I'm trying to think how many black guys were in the truck. Fish cakes, Elton Fisher; I think that's it. I think Fish Cakes was the only black guy in the house. Twelve Engine had Curtiss Moore, Boisy Cosby, and Calvin Jackson. There was a forth guy, but I can't remember who it was. And they had Jimmy Finucan was their captain. It was pretty much white. Most of the guys that I hung around with were all white.

Ethnically, I would say Irish, German, and then some Italians. Wayne Rosetti worked with me in Twelve Engine. He was Italian. The captain, Rick Connell, of course was Irish. Charlie De Lillo was Italian. So, yes, it was a mix.

Pignato: Well, let's see the captain of the engine was a Sceppaguercio, there's an Ippolito, and on the truck there was a Gaguski and my captain was DePaul. There were half Italians in the place. But I told everyone I wasn't Italian. I was Sicilian. There were also Irish and German, a couple of black guys.

Perdon: When I was appointed the department was Irish and Italian. There were a handful of minorities, a handful. There weren't many at all. You had Richie Freeman. You had Willie Webb, Lowell Jones, Calvin Jackson; really, there were only a handful.

Chapter Six: Hours and Salary

Fredette: We worked eighty-four hours a week for twenty one hundred dollars a year. I worked with Chief Ruscheck. I got him two days and two nights. He was like on my shift. When I worked two tens I would get Ruscheck. Then when I worked the twenty-four, I would go over on the other shift, the second platoon, and then I would have a different chief and a different captain. Two of us would go over and work with the guys on the other shift. After putting in that twenty-four, we would have to come back and do fourteens with our original shift. Then we would be off a day. That was the schedule then two ten-hour days, the twenty-four, two fourteen hour nights, and a day off.

There was always one guy on your shift you worked steady with. The other four men we didn't get every day. We had a two-piece company, so we had six men. There was only one guy on my shift that I worked with steady. We would both go over on the other shift. We got to know everybody. It was not like today. You don't get a chance to know people. We got to know everybody because everybody naturally got a chance to work with each other.

Vetrini: We worked seventy-two hours a week. One day eight to six, then the next day you would work a twenty four, the next day you would work a fourteen hour night, and then another fourteen hour night. Then you would change your crew. You would wind up working an eight to six, a twenty-four, and then only one fourteen. But that only came every so many shifts that you would pick up that free day. They called it a Kelly day at that time. The Captain always had at least two of his men working, but sometimes you would be working with the other Captain. When you worked a twenty-four, you would pick up the other Captain. The Captain would work his twenty-four with his two drivers. Because when you were a driver, you were THE driver. There was no such thing as he would switch and let you drive that apparatus. The only time you would drive that apparatus was when the first driver was off. At the time when I went on as a temporary we were making twenty-one hundred a year. Then we went up to about twenty four hundred. That's where it was in nineteen fifty-one when I brought a house. Ninety-three dollars every two weeks was our check.

Redden: As I remember it now we worked two days, then a twenty-four, two nights, and then you're off twenty-four. When you worked the twenty-four, you got a couple hour meal trick. Then every once in a while, to even things out as far as hours were concerned, you got a Kelly day. I thoroughly enjoyed it. My brother, at that time, was on the Police Department and they were working, I believe, a forty-eight hour week. I was working an eighty-four and I was home more than he was. If I had a decent night in the firehouse, the next day I'm foot loose and fancy free. So, it was great. Of course, when you did that twenty-four, you switched from one captain to the other. There were two captains, two platoons. The salary when I came on was twenty-four hundred to thirty-three hundred. Thirty-three was the top salary. That was over a three year period.

Kinnear: The hours at that time were seventy-two hours a week and one of the days was a twenty-four hour day. You got a two-hour dinner break sometime during the day. The hours went back to eighty-four hours for a very short time. I think for a month right after I got on the job. Basically you worked three days. The third day was your twenty-four. You also worked that night. Then you worked three nights including the twenty-four. Then you would have one twenty-four hour period off before the cycle started again. Once in a while they'd give you what they called a Kelly day, an extra day off. Then in '49 we went to the fifty-six hour week. That was two days, two nights, and two days off. In '59 we went to forty-two hours.

When I first went on the job the salary was twenty-four hundred a year. That, of course, was the low range for the salary. The top range for a full grade fireman was thirty-three hundred a year. It took four years to get here.

Masters: We worked eighty-four hours a week, twenty-four hundred dollars a year. And if they had an emergency, they would keep you there as long as they wanted. You didn't get paid for it either. There was no comp time. Especially in the winter, I remember one year the whole city was paralyzed, in '47. The cars were abandoned in the streets. Trolley cars weren't running and they held you there, they held you there for as long as they wanted. You didn't get paid for it.

Grehl: In 1947 they were working eighty-four hours, but as soon as they got the people on the job, they cut it to seventy-two and that's what I worked, seventy-two. To cut the hours they gave you what they called a Kelly day. Every once in a while you would get an extra day off when you more or less accumulated time in excess of what the working days were. They would give you a Kelly day, a day that you would get that extra ten hours, so you didn't work more than the seventy two. It didn't last very long when I was on the job. When I got on there were very, very few. By that time they were starting to fill the rolls. A year later they had them pretty well filled up.

There were still only two tours when I came on the fire department, but because they had some increased manpower we were able to work a twenty-four hour period. Because we worked that twenty-four hour period that gave fellows time off so they could go from an eighty-four to a seventy-two hour work period. Then maybe a year later they went into a sixty-four hour work period. At that period we cut out that twenty-four workday. They could do it because of these new men from the 1947 and '48 list working in the fire department. It wasn't until 1949 that we went to the fifty-six hour work week, which started the three tours. We stayed at that until 1959 when we went to the forty-two hour work week, which is what they're working now.

Vesey: We worked three days and four nights; then you had a seventy-two. Then you reversed, four days and three nights. It went like that until the fifty-six hours.

McCormack: The third tour just came in when I was appointed. We were making twenty-four hundred dollars a year to start. Top salary was thirty-six hundred. The working fireman was barely at subsistence level.

Masterson: They started the fifty-six hours. I went on with the fifty-six. I think they had the eighty-four hours before that. Then they went to the fifty-six hours. When I came on they started the third tour. That was the beginning of the third tour. Then later on they went to fourth tour. We worked two days and two nights. Then you were off two days. It was a six day schedule.

I made twenty-five hundred dollars a year, not a week, a year, not even a month. That's why everybody worked part time. We were always below school teachers then. In fact, when I went on it took you four years for full seniority. The starting salary was always less, but then every year you got an increase and you became full grade. That was what the younger guys were complaining about. They were doing all the work. The job didn't pay. Twenty-five hundred dollars a year, before I came on it was twenty-four hundred dollars a year. Your check was paid the first and the fifteenth. So, I think I got seventy-eight dollars one pay and I got seventy-two dollars the next pay. I remember the first year I filed my income tax in Ten Engine. A guy used to come around the firehouses and prepare income taxes. The captain made three thousand dollars that year and that year I was driving for Pepsi Cola. For the ten months I worked in Pepsi Cola I made more money than the captain.

Deutch: We worked fifty-six hours, two days, two nights, two off. I started with twenty-four hundred dollars in 1953 and the officers were getting like six hundred more.

Wall: We were working fifty-six hours then. It was still ten-hour days, fourteen-hour nights, but you put in two days, got a swing then put in two nights then you had two days off. You didn't have a full day off in between the days and the nights. As I recall you had two ten-hour days, so you went off at six o'clock, then you went back on the following night at six o'clock for two nights. Then you had two full days off.

But to me that was a break because the year I was on the cops, I worked night patrol. And you literally worked some time every day of the week because you worked a shift. You'd come on duty something like nine o'clock at night, went off at five in the morning. But your first night in, you came in at midnight. It's called the dogwatch. You worked from midnight until eight in the morning. At that time there were no unions to speak of. There was the PBA, but they weren't very effective. They made you come in fifteen minutes, twenty minutes before your shift started on your own time for your roll call or what have you. So, if looked at a calendar, every day you were in the police precinct for some period of time.

In 1959, the forty-two hour week came in and they created the fourth tour. There was all sort of jockeying for position if you were first driver or first tiller man. They tried to re-assign the experienced guys so the fourth tour wouldn't be all new people. Everybody was trying to avoid going to "F" Troop at the time. No one wanted to go to a new tour.

I think we came on at something like three thousand five hundred dollars a year. At that time there were ten steps between recruit and fireman first grade. The first year I was on or even before I was sworn in, there was a referendum where we got a five hundred dollar raise. I actually came on at four thousand dollars a year. At that time we were part of the Department of Public Safety. John B. Keenan was the director. We were the Division of Fire or the Division of Police. So, we had parity with the Police. We have always been at parity. We maintained parity with the officer ranks, too.

McGee: The salary was four thousand a year. I believe it had just gone to four thousand and they had just come down to fifty-six hours a year or two previously. So I started at fifty-six hours a week.

Stoffers: We were working fifty-six hours a week. When they felt that the forty-two was going to go in then they started building up the companies. So that when it came time for the forty-two, they wouldn't have that much of an impact on the budget. We filled up spots that were already vacant. Companies were assigned one officer and five or six men.

McGrory: You worked two days ten hours, two nights fourteen hours, forty-eight hours off and then right back again. It was only forty-eight hours off. You went off that morning and forty-eight hours from then you came back. So it was a fifty-six hour week. One time early on in the century they only had one tour. A guy would get maybe one day off in seven and they'd get meal tricks. Some of the old timers used to talk about meal tricks and everything like that. When I first came on the job there were still quite a few of the old timers.

I think the salary was forty-five hundred a year. Everybody thought in the city that firemen and cops got their uniforms, their turn out gear, and their kids had everything paid for. They didn't. You paid towards your hospitalization. You bought all your uniforms. You bought all your turnout gear. That was it. I took a cut. I was making quite a bit more than that in Otis, but I couldn't see myself staying there. I tell you the happiest thing I ever did was go on the fire department.

Denvir: The salary was forty-five hundred when I came on in 1959 and we worked forty-two hours. Then I think the next July we got a raise up to five thousand.

Carragher: It was forty-five hundred dollars when I came on. The salary was forty-five hundred to start; fifty-four was top pay. There was maybe six hundred dollars difference in the ranks at the time. A captain was six hundred more than a fireman, a Battalion six hundred more than him, and a Deputy six hundred more than him.

Harris: I believe it was around forty-five hundred dollars. Of course you had all the benefits and everything that went with it, plus your salary, so you were doing rather well. I was just starting out my family, so that was good for me.

Haran: The salary was forty five hundred a year to six thousand. It took you five years to get there. You had a three hundred dollar raise each year. I worked in the phone company. I was making a hundred and nine fifty a week, working thirty-five hours a week, off at night, off on Saturdays and Sundays. Holidays were off. I started with forty five hundred dollars a year which is approximately eighty-two dollars a week, eighty-two fifty. We were working forty-two hours a week. I took a cut in pay. I was working nights. I was working weekends. We didn't get paid for any holidays and we weren't off on any holidays unless the schedule fell that way. My father thought I was nuts. He said, "What the hell did I raise here? I thought I raised somebody with a little sense."

Highsmith: When I came on the job the salary was eighty-five hundred and then in a few years we fought for raises. We went to ten-five. I had just left the Post Office. This job would give me about a two thousand dollar a year raise. I was really rolling in the money.

Cody: I started on the fire department at fifty-one hundred and ten dollars. It was a step up, but not much. It was pretty close. I was on not too long, we went to fifty-six hundred, but the hours were better than bus driving. You had to drive a bus to realize that.

McGovern: I took a pay cut from my job at Western Electric. But I couldn't stand it there. I was on the night shift. In the morning it took me over a half hour to forty-five minutes just to get out of the parking lot. There were so many people working there and I couldn't stand it. So, I was ready to take any job.

I started at six thousand seven hundred and fifty nine dollars. After you made full grade we went to eight thousand. Then I think it was 1970, we picketed Trenton and went to ten five which was unheard of. Wow, nobody makes ten five. That was a big deal at that time. Everybody showed up and we marched on Trenton and the bill was passed. Everybody got ten five. I think it was three years to make full grade fireman at the time. I went from six seven five nine to eight thousand within three years. And then shortly after that we went to ten five.

Prachar: When I came on in '68 it was seventy-five hundred. A year later everybody was going to quit their part-time jobs because we were getting a twenty-five hundred dollar raise and we went to ten thousand. Thought it was great. I went home. I told my wife we were going to buy a new car. I'm getting this big salary.

But back then you loved the job. You didn't come to the job for the salary. You came to the job because you wanted to do the job. But now I can't live on seventy-five hundred for a month. You start thinking what you pay for your house, your insurance. I put two kids through college. Seventy-five hundred just would not have made it. That was tough, but you did it because you loved the job.

Cosby: The salary at that time was eight thousand five hundred. Which wasn't a lot of money at that time, but it went a lot further. The mortgage on my house in Newark at that time was only eighty dollars a month. I had purchased the house for nine thousand five hundred. So it wasn't a lot of money, but it went a lot further than the salary goes today.

Pianka: I thought it was great. I left a job earning six-five. I went to a job earning nine-five to start. After a year I went up to ten-five. So, I couldn't complain. I thought it was great. I give those guys a lot of credit. They went out on strike, took a risk to get a raise. They didn't leave the new guys coming on out in the cold. We all got that raise together. That's why when I came on the job I started at nine-five. They didn't say, "Well, we want nine-five, but the guys coming on, let them come on at six-five. I guess we were union men. Even though we weren't organized as much as we are in now days, we all went together.

McDonnell: It was nine thousand five hundred which was from the raise they got the year when they had the strike. I forget what the raise was. I think they got twenty-five hundred dollars in the raise which was like a third of what they were making. It wasn't really that good. At that time they thought it was a lot of money. My brother told me, "You'll have more money than you'll know what to do with."

Rotonda: When I came on in 1970 I was making about twelve thousand a year at Coca-Cola. I also had four children when I came on this job and my wife was pregnant for my fifth. This job started you out at eight thousand or eighty-five hundred. That kind of money is a big amount to makeup. That's the only thing I was worried about. That was a little scary at that time. You're talking about a four thousand dollar difference roughly. Four thousand is a lot of money when you're talking between a top of twelve thousand dollars. You could buy a house for ten thousand dollars at that time. It was a little scary. It worked out fortunately, but that was a big difference.

T. Grehl: It started at nine-five; then you went to ten thousand and then ten-five. It was in steps and it changed every January. So I came on in

August of '71 at nine-five and made ten thousand January first and then the following year it became ten thousand five hundred. At that time they had just gotten a two thousand, twenty-five hundred dollar influx of money from the State of New Jersey. That was during the Addonizio era. They just went up from that. So prior to that, they were making eight thousand or eighty-five. I think '70 is when they got the raise.

Ryan: My grandfather, when he came on they were working two shifts and he was allowed to go home for meal breaks. The hours were very long. The third shift coming in right after the Second World War and the fourth was after he retired. My dad started on the fire department in 1947.

The salary when I started was ninety-six hundred dollars. As a federal firefighter and having been promoted, I was making two thousand dollars less than that working seventy-two hours an week. So, it was a considerable increase in time off and in pay.

Langenbach: Well, when I came out of the service I said, "If I ever find a job that pays ten thousand dollars a year, I'm set." Well, I came on the job here, I made eight two fifty to start and then we got the big raise. 1974, we got the big raise, a twenty-five hundred dollar kick. I went to ten thousand, ten two-fifty. That was it. I was set. I didn't have to go anyplace else.

Luxton: I remember when I went on in Nutley, it was September 21, 1970 and Newark had just gotten to ten five. Nutley was something less than that. I know I started at sixty-two hundred in Nutley. It might have been ten thousand by that time. It was a couple of years later and maybe starting pay for firemen had gone close to ten or ninety-five. Something along those lines, something like that. Because I remember thinking, "Yeah, gee ten five, never made ten thousand dollars a year." I think the steps were closer together. You didn't have an eight or six thousand dollar range. You might have gotten a five hundred dollar raise. That was a big number.

Connell: I was making five hundred dollars more in Newark than I was in Passaic. So in 1974 I'm starting at ten-five. There were three steps to full grade which I believe was around twelve thousand. Within the first year we got a thousand dollar raise. When we came on, toll collectors on the Turnpike and the Parkway were making fifteen hundred dollars more a year than we were. But it always struck me, what am I doing here putting my life on the line? I could be on the Parkway collecting coins and making more money, but fortunately I fell in love with the job.

Pignato: Let's see, it was a cut in pay for me, I believe. I worked for the New Jersey Natural Gas Company before I came here. I was a first class pipe fitter. Came here, it was probably a five hundred dollar cut in pay. But I figured it was probably going to get better. The hours were better. So, it was ten thousand, eleven thousand dollars, something like that.

Langevin: I started at eleven thousand three hundred dollars. I was making dirt working for the phone company. I think I was bringing home ninety-one dollars a week with the phone company. With the eleven thousand three hundred dollars, my first paycheck for two weeks was like three hundred and seventy five dollars. I thought I was rich.

Perdon: We were making, I think it was over ten thousand dollars. It might have been over ten thousand, because I was making about nine when I was in the Post Office and then I got a raise. It was about ten thousand, eleven thousand, in that area.

Bisogna: Twelve thousand five hundred the first year. Six months later we went to fourteen five or so. We got a pretty good increase. It was every year you went up a step because January was the date, so six months later January came. We went to fourteen five. The next January we might have gone to seventeen and then maybe to twenty-one or two. In three or four years on the job we were making the low twenties. I don't recall the exact numbers. It was enough to get by. You weren't getting rich, but at that time my rent was two hundred a month.

Back then you couldn't put your kids in better schools and stuff like that. I lived in Newark. My father was on the job. When they went on strike in '70, he went from eight thousand five hundred to ten thousand. That was a big deal. I don't know how he put shoes on our feet. He always worked another job. That's how he did it. My mother didn't work either, so it wasn't easy.

Ricca: When I came on, it was twelve thousand five hundred and fifty dollars, I believe. And it had just jumped from eight thousand. But I know that the cadets at the time were making five thousand and that's why I didn't take the cadet test. I had the opportunity to take it. I came out of the air conditioning school, I was making fifteen five. At the time, I was interested in the firehouse, but not completely thinking I wanted to be a fireman. I had given thoughts to becoming a cop, but only entertained it, never even seriously pursued it. And I liked what I did. I liked doing the air conditioning.

Gesualdo: Initially, we worked the two ten hour days followed by a swing day and then two fourteen hour nights followed by seventy-two hours off. The initial salary I remember like it was yesterday, fourteen thousand seven hundred dollars. When you have two kids and a wife and you're looking to buy a house, those numbers stick in your head. I was actually making quite good money with Public Service as a lineman, but my wife had some problems with homesickness. She was born in England and lived there until she was eighteen. I had no option but really to go back, take her home for a while. So, coming back in the middle '70's, during the Carter years, inflation rates were up. Interest rates were up. Jobs were scarce. You had to take what you can get.

I remember it being very depressing knowing what I had been earning compared to what I was earning. Fortunately I had a home before we moved to England and reinvested my money there in a home. Then we came back, sold the home in England, so I had enough finances to buy another home. I didn't really feel like I was destitute. But it was probably lower middle income at that point.

List of Interviewees

Baldino, Captain Barney, letter to the author 20 September, 2002. (appointed 1951)

Belzger, Firefighter William, 4 October, 2004, transcript. (appointed 1959)

Bisogna, Captain Joseph, 25 July, 2001, transcript. (appointed 1974)

Butler, Captain James, 3 September 1993, transcript. (appointed 1963)

Cahill, Firefighter Joseph, 25 June 1991, transcript. (appointed 1963)

Carragher, Deputy Chief William, November 1994, transcript. (appointed 1960)

Carter, Battalion Chief Harry, 12 June, 1991, transcript. (appointed 1973)

Charpentier, Firefighter Frederick, 22 August 1993, transcript. (appointed 1959)

Cody, Battalion Chief James, 26 October 1999, transcript. (appointed 1964)

Connell, Battalion Chief Anthony, 26 February, 1999, 24 November, 2003. (appointed 1974)

Cosby, Firefighter Joseph, 22 August, 1991, transcript. (appointed 1969)

Denvir, Captain John, 13 September 1993, transcript. (appointed 1959)

Deutch, Firefighter Charles, 14 November 1993, transcript. (appointed 1953)

Dunn, Deputy Chief Edward, 14 August 1991, 29 August 1997, transcript. (appointed 1959)

Finucan, Deputy Chief James, 7 August 1991, transcript. (appointed 1969)

Freda, Deputy Chief Alfred, 12, 25, 26 July 1991, transcript. (appointed 1959)

Fredette, Firefighter Reggie, 3 November, 1993, transcript. (appointed 1942)

Freeman, Captain Richard, 20, 21 August 1991, transcript. (appointed 1956)

Garrity, Battalion Chief Joseph, May 1992, transcript. (appointed 1964)

Gesualdo, Captain Al, 21 July, 2003, transcript. (appointed 1978)

Grehl, Deputy Chief Frederick, 7 August 1993, transcript. (appointed 1948)

Grehl, Captain Thomas, 29 May, 2002, transcript. (appointed 1971)

Griffith, Chief Fire Alarm Operator Robert, 3 July, 1991, transcript. (appointed 1953)

Haran, Captain Edward, 5 February 2001, transcript. (appointed 1961)

Harris, Captain William, 13 December 1999, transcript. (appointed 1961)

Highsmith, Firefighter Gerald, 2 June 1994, transcript. (appointed 1963)

Kinnear, Deputy Chief David, 28 September 1992, transcript. (appointed 1947)

Knight, Firefighter Gerald, 19 June 1991, transcript. (appointed 1964)

Langenbach, Deputy Chief James, 24 October, 2002, transcript. (appointed 1973)

Langevin, Firefighter Robert, 23 February, 1999, transcript. (appointed 1974)

Luxton, Captain Charles, 14 January, 1999, transcript. (appointed 1973)

Marcell, Firefighter Andrew, 23 September 1998, transcript. (appointed 1959)

Masters, Firefighter Anthony, 24 March, 2004, transcript. (appointed 1947)

Masterson, Captain Andrew, 6 April, 2005, transcript. (appointed 1949)

McCormack, Sr. Deputy Chief James, 14 June 1991, transcript. (appointed 1949)

McDonnell, Captain Thomas, 30 March, 1999, 16 April, 1999, transcript. (appointed 1970)

McGee, Captain Raymond, 26 October 2000, transcript. (appointed 1956)

McGovern, Battalion Chief Thomas, 8 June, 2001, transcript. (appointed 1968)

McGrory. Deputy Chief Albert, 31 August 1991, transcript. (appointed 1957)

Melodick, Firefighter William, June, 2001, transcript. (appointed 1970)

Miller, Battalion Chief Joseph, 16, 21 August 1991, transcript. (appointed 1959)

Perdon, Captain George, 9 June, 2003, transcript. (appointed 1974)

Pianka, Firefighter George, 15 June, 2001, transcript. (appointed 1970)

Pignato, Captain Nicholas, 26 May, 1999, transcript. (appointed 1974)

Prachar, Captain Daniel, 12 August, 1991, transcript. (appointed 1968)

Redden, Fire Chief Joseph, 16 September 2002, transcript. (appointed 1947)

Ricca, Battalion Chief Ronald, 1 June, 2000, transcript. (appointed 1974)

Rotonda, Firefighter Gerard, 3 May, 2000, transcript. (appointed 1970)

Ryan, Battalion Chief Joseph, 28 September, 1999, transcript. (appointed 1973)

Smith, Firefighter James, 2 September 1998, transcript. (appointed 1959)

Stoffers, Battalion Chief Carl, 2 September 1998, transcript. (appointed 1956)

Vesey, Firefighter Edward, 15 June 1999, transcript. (appointed 1948)

Vetrini, Captain Joseph, 14 September, 1993, transcript. (appointed 1946)

Wall, Deputy Chief Edward, 13 September, 2000, transcript. (appointed 1954)

Wargo, Captain Andrew, 6 June 1991, transcript. (appointed 1964)